HOW A PASTOR WITH GAY PARENTS
LEARNED TO LOVE OTHERS
WITHOUT SACRIFICING CONVICTION

MESSY GRACE

CALEB KALTENBACH
FOREWORD BY KYLE IDLEMAN

WATERBROOK
PRESS

MESSY GRACE
PUBLISHED BY WATERBROOK PRESS
12265 Oracle Boulevard, Suite 200
Colorado Springs, Colorado 80921

All Scripture quotations are taken from the Holy Bible, New International Version®, NIV®. Copyright © 1973, 1978, 1984, 2011 by Biblica Inc.™ Used by permission of Zondervan. All rights reserved worldwide. www.zondervan.com.

Italics in Scripture quotations reflect the author's added emphasis.

Details in some anecdotes and stories have been changed to protect the identities of the persons involved.

Trade Paperback ISBN 978-1-60142-736-6
eBook ISBN 978-1-60142-737-3

Cover design by Kristopher K. Orr; cover photography by Shawn Marshall, 500px

Published in the United States by WaterBrook Multnomah, an imprint of the Crown Publishing Group, a division of Penguin Random House LLC, New York.

WATERBROOK and its deer colophon are registered trademarks of Penguin Random House LLC.

Library of Congress Cataloging-in-Publication Data
Kaltenbach, Caleb.
    Messy grace : how a pastor with gay parents learned to love others without sacrificing conviction / Caleb Kaltenbach. — First edition.
        pages cm
    ISBN 978-1-60142-736-6 (paperback) — ISBN 978-1-60142-737-3 (electronic)
1. Homosexuality—Religious aspects—Christianity. 2. Interpersonal relations—Religious aspects—Christianity. 3. Sexual minorities. 4. Sex—Religious aspects—Christianity. 5. Christian life. I. Title.
    BR115.H6K35 2015
    248.4—dc23
                                            2015012987

Printed in the United States of America
2016

10 9 8 7 6 5 4

SPECIAL SALES
Most WaterBrook Multnomah books are available at special quantity discounts when purchased in bulk by corporations, organizations, and special-interest groups. Custom imprinting or excerpting can also be done to fit special needs. For information, please e-mail SpecialMarkets@WaterBrookMultnomah.com or call 1-800-603-7051.

exhortation both to treat gay people lovingly and to hold true to one's convictions is winsome and challenging. His wisdom flows from life, being raised by two gay parents, coming to Christ, and sharing Christ's love with his parents and loved ones."

—JENELL PARIS, PHD, professor of anthropology at Messiah
College and author of *The End of Sexual Identity*

"This is an important conversation for the church today, and no one's story makes them better suited for it than Caleb Kaltenbach. In a world that tries to force everyone to take sides, Caleb speaks from the inside of both worlds. Gay or straight, Christian or non-Christian, everyone can learn from and be impacted by *Messy Grace*."

—LANE JONES, director of Strategic Partners at North Point
Ministries and co-author of *Communicating for a Change*

"*Messy Grace* is a wonderful, well-written, and highly readable account of the author's remarkable journey being raised in the gay community and how he came to faith. Caleb provides insightful guidance to churches and families dealing with LGBT issues that goes beyond the worn-out platitudes that have characterized this discussion for some time."

—SCOTT B. RAE, PHD, dean of faculty and professor of Christian ethics at Talbot School of Theology, Biola University

"With uncompromising conviction, Kaltenbach teaches each one of us to hear the heart of God and to be the face of Christ in a broken world. The call for mercy, love, grace, and compassion are written on every page and are both highly courageous and poignantly raw."

—MICHELLE ANTHONY, author of *Spiritual Parenting*
and *Becoming a Spiritually Healthy Family*

"Pastor Kaltenbach gives his readers much help on what to do and what not to do among LGBT people. At the same time, he recognizes and emphasizes that this is a messy world, and that God calls us to affirm Jesus in the midst of the messiness, rather than to expect a precise answer to every question."

—Dr. JOHN FRAME, J. D. Trimble professor of systematic theology
and philosophy at Reformed Theological Seminary

"I loved *Messy Grace*! These pages are filled with humility, compassion, and powerful insights as Caleb's story profoundly demonstrates that grace is both messy and beautiful."

—MIKE FOSTER, People of the Second Chance

"Whether you are straight or part of the LGBT community, a Christian or not a follower of Jesus, it will benefit you to read this book. Prepare to be challenged. Prepare to repent. Prepare to be changed. It will transform the way you look at and treat others. I couldn't put it down."

—DANIEL AKIN, president of Southeastern Baptist
Theological Seminary

"Real, relevant, and relational—*Messy Grace* steps right into the existing chasm between the Christian community and the gay community and provides the sound biblical direction about how the gospel is the grounds for how we can mend and connect in a Christ-honoring way."

—BRYAN CARTER, senior pastor of Concord Church,
Dallas, Texas

"Caleb Kaltenbach has seen both sides of this controversial and complex topic . . . from his parents and from his pulpit. While it's tough for everyone to agree on such delicate issues, Caleb takes us back to Scripture."

—DAVE STONE, senior pastor of Southeast Christian Church,
Louisville, Kentucky

"The church needs to get this issue right. *Messy Grace* is an outstanding book that every Christian needs to read. Not only will you enjoy Caleb's casual and humorous writing style; you will be challenged to live in grace and truth, just like Jesus."

—SEAN MCDOWELL, PHD, professor at Biola University, popular
speaker, and the co-author of over fifteen books, including
Same-Sex Marriage

"Caleb shares his story with a leader's wisdom, a preacher's convictions, and a pastor's tender heart. When I talk with families (and churches) wrestling with how to love someone who is gay, I will put this book in their hands."

—MATT PROCTOR, president of Ozark Christian College

"I have known Caleb for many years and know of no one more imminently qualified to address the single most controversial subject of our day and to do so with love and grace. Sharing his challenges as a son of gay parents and his convictions as a servant of Christ will keep you engaged to the very last page."

— BARRY CAMERON, senior pastor of Crossroads Christian Church

"Caleb fluently speaks both the language and the emotion of both sides of the issue. And he desperately wants to help us stop picking sides and learn to love like Jesus. He is a great leader, writer, and friend — as well as a walking example of how messy grace works."

— Dr. TIM HARLOW, senior pastor of Parkview Christian Church

"Finally a book on a divisive issue that is handled with grace and truth. Caleb has seen both sides of the issue firsthand, and his counsel is something the church today needs to hear. This is a must-read for pastors and church leaders."

— DON WILSON, senior pastor of Christ's Church of the Valley

"Pastor Caleb Kaltenbach's story is one of pain and alienation, pride and determination, brokenness and eventually the healing love of Jesus Christ. This powerful book is a must-read for both Christians and non-Christians alike."

— FRANK SONTAG, host of *The Frank Sontag Show* on 99.5 KKLA

"Few books will challenge your head and your heart like *Messy Grace*. It embodies a rare combination of grace and truth and serves as a beautiful reminder that Jesus died for all people. It is poignant, practical, and personal."

— JON WEECE, author of *Jesus Prom*

To my wife—
I love you so much. Not only are you God's great
treasure to me, but you're the best person I know.

To my son and daughter—
You will be ten times the disciples for Jesus
that I am. I'm proud of you. I love you.

To my parents—
I would not be who I am without you. This
conversation wouldn't be happening without you.
I'm thankful to be your son.

To Larry and Norma—
Thank you for loving me. Your support and love
are so encouraging.

To Sean and Jonina—
I'm no longer an only child. I love you both
and love being your brother.

Contents

Foreword

first met Caleb in college. He was a freshman, and I was a junior. He came with very little knowledge of the Bible (he was a new Christian), but he possessed a huge love for God and people. I saw Caleb as someone eager to learn about God and to make a difference in the world.

One day we were both sitting outside a professor's office, waiting to talk to him about a class. I asked Caleb how he came to Bible college and sat in disbelief as he told me about himself. I had never heard a story like that before.

After graduation, Caleb and I were on staff together at a church in Los Angeles. There we started an alternative worship service for young adults. During that time, I watched Caleb deepen his love for God and people. Because of his childhood experiences, he was able to relate with those who disdained Christians. He understood what it was like to be angry at God for the way believers treated others. God certainly used Caleb's experiences to touch the hearts of many people. Now, after knowing him for twenty years, I'm still blown away by how God continues to write this story.

Throughout the years I've encouraged Caleb to share his story with as many people as he can. Many of us have told him again and again to write it down. Today, I'm proud that you're holding it in your hands. Such messy grace takes great courage to share.

Some authors have inspirational stories to tell, while others have insightful points to make. What makes Caleb's writing so powerful is that God has given him both. You'll read about a boy who was raised in the LGBT community, who later followed Jesus. You'll read about how some Christians hated people he loved, and how his coming to faith wrecked his own relationships. You'll read about how Christians can hold true to what God says about sexuality while being gracious and loving.

If you think this story is just about a kid from the LGBT community, then you've missed the bigger point. It's about how we love people who are different from us. It's about how any story can be redeemed by God. It's about the messiness of grace and truth.

When you read this book, you may not agree with everything Caleb says, but you'll see his heart for people on both sides of the issue. I've been personally impacted by what God has done through Caleb and his family. I know you will be too.

—KYLE IDLEMAN, author of *Not a Fan* and teaching pastor
     at Southeast Christian Church, Louisville, Kentucky

A Collision of Communities

For a couple of minutes after I pulled into the church parking lot, I continued to sit in my Ford Escape, my hands gripping the steering wheel as if I were still driving. I hadn't turned the car off yet. Maybe I could back up and attend church down the road. I mean, did I really have to preach a sermon today?

I closed my eyes and tried to imagine I was somewhere else, maybe the beach or Disneyland. I wished it were some other time than now. But wishing did no good. I was actually here, in the parking lot of the church in Dallas that I was pastor of at the time. This was the Sunday morning in September 2012 I had been dreading for weeks.

After a while, I turned off the ignition, but I stayed seated in the car. People were pulling into the parking lot around me and heading into the building. Everyone in the church was expecting me to come in and deliver a sermon. What they didn't know was that I was feeling nervous about preaching this day. *Really* nervous. Generally, I'm very comfortable with preaching, but I was having an anxiety attack about this particular message.

Most Sundays, after the sermon, I was bound to hear comments like "That was a good one, Pastor," or "You sure let 'em have it," or "I never thought of those passages in that light." Today, none of those comments would mean anything. Regardless of what I said this morning, someone was bound to get hurt.

I got out of the car, grabbed my bag, and hurried toward the church.

After entering the building through the front doors, I had to slow down because I was greeted by a group of church members in the lobby. I put on my church face and shook hands, hugged people, and told them what a great day it was going to be. I laughed at jokes and reminisced about when the Cowboys were a good team.

As soon as I could politely break away from the crowd, I jogged down the hallway toward my office door. I unlocked it, turned on the light, and collapsed in a chair. A small part of the morning was past me, but the worst was still to come.

Immediately, thoughts began swirling in my head: *How did I get into this? How can I be sure God led me to this day? What kind of a moron would plan a Sunday like this?*

Oh yeah, me.

Every August I plan the sermon calendar for the following twelve months. During the most recent planning period, I knew that a presidential election was coming up in November. So I thought that for the fall it would be a good idea to do a sermon series dealing with some political issues from a biblical standpoint. We called the series "For or Against." The idea was to communicate to the congregation that our church should be known for what we are for, not what we're against.

When autumn rolled around, many people loved the series, but there were also critics. The funniest criticism I got was from a woman who complained about the series poster. One side of the poster had a red background with a thumbs-up image on it, and the other side had a blue background with a thumbs-down. Her complaint was that because we had a thumbs-down on the blue side, we were taking a stand against the Democrats. I assured her that I and the guys who designed the poster had no political bashing in mind. She grudgingly accepted my assurance—I think.

Today's sermon, however, would bring a whole new set of critics to the table. The title of this day's sermon was "For or Against Different Lifestyles."

I was preaching about homosexuality.

Yeah, let me say it one more time: that was *my* idea. Back in August, it had seemed perfect. Today I wanted to go back and punch Caleb-from-a-month-ago and yell "What in the world were you thinking?!" because he was forcing me to preach on a subject that was not only difficult in general but also hard for me on a personal level.

As I sat in my office, I could hear the worship music start in the auditorium. I waited through the first two songs. They seemed to be going by too quickly. Was the worship pastor intentionally speeding up the songs? At the beginning of the third song, I got up from the chair, grabbed a water bottle and my Bible, and headed toward the door.

Backstage, I put on my mic and stood there, trying to return the smiles of those around me, until I heard the last song.

It was time.

I felt my heart pounding, my stomach jumping, and sweat forming. So I closed my eyes and prayed: *Lord, you're the one who called me into ministry and to this place. You're the one who allowed me to have the experiences I did. You've been forming me and shaping me, and now I am so nervous to proclaim what I know I need to. Give me the confidence and power to do what I must.*

Why was I so nervous? Partly because some of the church members might object to what I was about to say. Partly because church elders tend to get nervous when sermons are too controversial. Partly because it was an election year and almost every sermon could be criticized for being too political. But even more than any of that, I was nervous because my parents were in the congregation on this day.

And both of my parents are gay.

The Invitation

Later in the book, I will tell you the outcome of the sermon I preached to my parents and all the others in attendance at church that Sunday in 2012. But to put it in perspective, I first need to tell you about some of the formative events I experienced over the many years leading up to one of the most nerve-racking sermons of my life. In this book I'm going to tell you my story of having a mom who was a lesbian and a dad who was gay, of growing up in the LGBT community with my mom and her partner, and of finding Christ and eventually becoming a pastor.[1] I'm also going to describe the path I took in coming to grips with what the Bible says about homosexuality and figuring out how to love and honor my parents in light of that teaching.

I'd like to say at the outset that I don't claim to be a great biblical scholar or brilliant theologian. I don't think my opinions are always right and everyone else's are wrong. I'm not writing this book to tell you what to think, but rather I hope that this book will spur you on to think more deeply on this issue for yourself, using the Bible as your chief guide. I'm sharing my experience as an insider to both the LGBT community and the Christian community, as well as giving you the insights I've gained.

Even though my personal story will make up a big part of this book, it really isn't about me at all. *It is about you.* I wrote this book for anyone who wants to know how to relate with grace and truth toward members of the LGBT community.

I'll give you a hint of what I said in my sermon that Sunday in September a few years ago: being unloving to gay people in your life is a sin. Also, it's a crying shame because it puts a barrier between people and the gospel. It's the opposite of being Christlike. I don't see Jesus acting like that anywhere in the Gospels.

> Jesus's command to "love your neighbor as yourself" does not have an exception clause for a gay "neighbor"—or, for that matter, any other "neighbor" we might find it hard to relate to.

Jesus's command to "love your neighbor as yourself" does not have an exception clause for a gay "neighbor"—or, for that matter, any other "neighbor" we might find it hard to relate to. Followers of Jesus have got to learn how to treat people in the LGBT community with love that has no limits and makes no compromises. We have to love people as Jesus does.

Is it easy? Will we always know what to say and do? Will we never be uncomfortable? Of course not. Even when Christians want to be gracious and kind to members of the LGBT community, we're not necessarily very good at it. Even when we do our best, others don't always react in a way we would desire. Sometimes relationships start at a low point and go down from there.

So let's admit it—it's going to be messy at times. Messiness is what happens when you try to live out God's perfect grace as a flawed person in a flawed world. Yet God has a way of working through us when we keep on trying to share his grace, regardless of how messy our situations get. That's why this book is titled *Messy Grace*—not because God is messy or a certain community is messy, but because *all* people are messy!

> Messiness is what happens when you try to live out God's perfect grace as a flawed person in a flawed world.

I'll be dealing much more with the mess and the glory of grace as we go on in this book. Right now, let me assure you . . .

This book is for you if you experience same-sex attraction, opposite-sex attraction, or some of both.

It's for you if you're sure the Bible condemns same-sex relationships, convinced the Bible permits it, or just plain confused on the point.

It is for you if you love Jesus, want to follow in his way, and want to know how to relate to people in the LGBT community in a way that honors him.

It's even for you if you just don't see what the big deal is. You may be thinking, *Why can't some Christians just leave the LGBT community alone and direct their energies toward bigger issues?* You'll find out.

If any of these categories describe you, then read on.

Why We're Grace Failures

The more Christians engage the LGBT community in a gracious way, the more genuine relationships will come from it. So, why aren't Christians better at getting along with the LGBT community?

I've often pondered why this might be. After all, we're followers of the most gracious man ever—Jesus. We've been the recipients of astounding, radical grace ourselves. We can hardly help reading about grace every time we open our favorite book. Yet all too often our reputation among the LGBT community for being ungracious is well deserved. Why?

I'm sure there are many reasons. Here are four of the most common ones.

Fear of the LGBT Community

Some Christians have different kinds of fears when they think about the LGBT community. For example, some fear that gay activism will wind up taking away Christians' rights. They believe that gay-favoring politics is becoming a means to limit how they can live, how they can do business, and even what they'll be allowed to legally say on the issue of homosexuality.

Will the worst predictions of religious restriction come to pass someday? I don't know. But even if they do, I know that God will be with us then just as he is now. He works strongly when his people come under different types of attacks. I also know that threats to our rights, whether real or merely dreaded, should not prevent us from showing the love and kindness that Jesus says we owe to all.

On a more personal level, some Christians are afraid because they think that those who are LGBT will be attracted to them. Now, this one has always cracked me up. Listen to me on this: if you're not attractive to the opposite sex, you're probably not attractive to the same sex. (I kid! I kid!) Seriously, we shouldn't worry about gay people making a move on us. Let's relax.

Lack of Biblical Understanding

A dirty little secret is that most Christians don't know the Bible very well. I would dare to say that most American Christians keep their Bible reading to about five minutes every month. They're familiar with a few favorite passages. The rest of the biblical landscape remains a vast unexplored territory to them.

Because of this lack of biblical understanding, Christians sense that they are not well prepared to have conversations about homosexuality and related issues. They're afraid they won't have the answers to hard questions that might be put to them. Or they're afraid they won't be able to back up their positions biblically, even if they're pretty sure they're right. They might get backed into a corner, make a mistake, or be made to look foolish.

Better not to engage the LGBT community at all, they figure, than do it badly. The result is that the Christian community is over here and some from the LGBT community are over there, and Christians look cold and distant.

I want to ask you this: If you're in this position, wouldn't it be better to learn your Bible and prepare yourself for this or any conversation that would arise?

And there is still another kind of lack of biblical understanding. Some Christians know the Bible inside and out; their lack of understanding comes not from absence of knowledge but from not knowing how to use their knowledge. Unfortunately, some Christians have used the Bible as a weapon to bludgeon those who disagree. This, too, is a lack of biblical understanding, as it shows no love toward those with differing worldviews.

Some Christians need to understand that we can be right in our beliefs but wrong in how we communicate them.

Absence of Empathy

Many Christians, I'm sorry to say, have never bothered to place themselves in the shoes of someone who is LGBT. What are the lives of gay people like? What are their needs and concerns? What are their dreams? How do others treat them? How do they feel about God and the church?

Let me tell you about one misconception that comes from not taking the time to understand gay people: many Christians think that homosexuality is mainly about sex. They believe that you're in the LGBT community because you want to have sex with people of the same gender. This isn't totally true. Sex is only a part of the equation (and probably a small part for some). Most Christians haven't thought this issue through enough to realize that there is more to someone who identifies as LGBT than sexuality—a lot more.

All people have experiences, history, beliefs, friends, family, and more that make them into the people they are. Or as I like to say, all people have *depth*. So when we reduce homosexuality to just sex, we are thinking in a way that is far too shallow. People are just not that simple. We ought to get to know them as they are.

Closed-Door Attitude

Then there are some Christians who know their stuff. These Christians understand a lot of the Bible, have attended numerous Bible studies or Sunday school classes, lead their own groups, attend conferences, go to marriage retreats, and more. They are full-on Christians. First, let me say that I love Christians who fit this description. I love them even more when they don't just go to events or classes to learn more but also put that learning into action by serving others. I want people in my church to do all of these things and to grow in their knowledge of the Bible—and it's even better when they use what they've learned to lead others to Jesus.

Unfortunately, some of these Christians (not all, but some) are the kind of Christians who tend to shut people out of their lives if they don't fit their brand of Christianity. As I'll share in the book, I've run into this type of Christian a lot in my life (even in churches that I've served in). There are times when these Christians can be so concerned about holiness that they end up keeping away those who are less than perfect. They create a church culture that allows only a narrow few to participate in the community. I don't think the majority of these Christians mean to do this or even know they are doing this to others. It comes from putting a huge emphasis on knowledge without loving those whom Jesus loved. Having the mind-set that you've got it together and everyone else is lacking is a fast track to being a grace failure.

> Having the mind-set that you've got it together and everyone else is lacking is a fast track to being a grace failure.

Because of these reasons and more, not all Christians know how to think critically or talk comfortably about the issue of homosexuality. And because of our failure to approach this issue on a deeper level, we often miss opportunities to dialogue with others. Worse, we end up hurting other people.

Now I want to tell you about a young man named Hector and an encounter he had with some Christians that deeply affected his views of himself and God.[2] As you read his story, try to imagine how he felt, because it's likely that someone you know has felt very much the same way.

What It's Like to Be Hector

"Guys, I've got something I want to tell you," Hector spoke up. A twenty-year-old Hispanic man attending Cal State Northridge in the Los Angeles area, Hector was with three other college-aged men, new friends of his, in the home belonging to the mom of one of the other guys. It was late on a Wednesday evening. They had finished watching a movie and were sitting in the family room, eating the last of the popcorn and talking and laughing together. A lot of the conversation had to do with girls in the college group at the church where these four friends had met.

Hector hoped the others didn't notice the slight tremor in his voice. They would never know how hard it was for him to bring up what he was about to say.

"What is it?" said Ryan. "Shoot."

"I don't know what you're going to think about this," Hector said, "but I'm actually into dudes."

Chewed bits of popcorn shot out of VJ's mouth as he started to laugh. Ryan and James both laughed too. They all thought Hector was kidding.

When Hector sat there looking serious and embarrassed, the laughing faltered. VJ coughed and then took a swallow of soda.

In the awkward silence that ensued, Ryan said to Hector, "Are you serious?"

"Yeah, man," Hector replied. "Is that so hard to believe?"

The other three guys glanced nervously at each other, and then each tried to put on a concerned, attentive face. They started asking Hector questions.

How long had Hector known this about himself?

Since a young age. He'd worked hard to keep it from his family, but he'd never been able to deny it to himself.

Had Hector been molested or mistreated?

No. He'd been raised just like his older and younger brothers, both of whom were straight. He'd never been babied by his mother or bullied by his father. No one had ever laid a hand on him in the wrong way when he was a kid.

Had he ever, you know . . . done stuff with a guy?

Ryan whacked VJ over the head with a sofa pillow for asking this question, and Hector didn't deign to answer it.

How did he think God felt about his same-sex attraction?

Hector had been an altar boy in the Catholic church his family attended when he was growing up, and whenever the priest talked about "the sin of homosexuality," he had felt ashamed and fearful of God's punishment. For a long time, he'd prayed almost daily for God to remove his attraction to other males, but it had never happened. When he went to college, he tried to forget about God and joined a partying crowd, many of whom were either LGBT or questioning their sexuality. When all the partying made him feel empty, he'd started attending the evangelical church where he'd met Ryan, James, and VJ. He wasn't sure if his sexual orientation was all right in God's eyes or not. He knew, though, that he was interested in Jesus again.

Why had Hector told the other guys this about himself?

Hector just thought they ought to know, if they were going to be friends.

At this point in the conversation, Hector was thinking that things had gone decently well. He was beginning to relax.

But then things fell apart.

James, who hadn't said much up to this point, started firing Bible verse after Bible verse at him. At first Hector tried to listen and take it as if James were genuinely trying to educate him on the Bible's view of marriage and intimacy. But quickly it began to feel like an attack, and Hector got mad.

Ryan said to James, "Cut it out! He doesn't need that right now."

Then Ryan turned to Hector and said, "Look, Hec, we can help. Do you want us to pray for God to release you from the demons of homosexuality?"

It was Hector's turn to laugh out loud before realizing Ryan was serious. "I don't think I can do this anymore right now," he suddenly said. "See you guys later." He grabbed his jacket and was out of there the next instant.

Hector went back to his dorm that night feeling defeated and unsure of whether he had made the right decision to tell his friends about being gay.

Over the next few days, no one from the church college group called him. That Sunday, when he went to church, the guys he usually hung out with were strangely cold toward him. He caught a couple of weird glances from other members of the college group too. The pastor of the group pulled him aside and said that he'd like to talk with him sometime that week. Hector knew. The rumors had spread.

That was Hector's last day at that church.

In fact, it was Hector's last day at any church for quite a while.

Living in the Tension

Unfortunately, as a pastor, I am all too familiar with stories like Hector's—stories where Christians had the chance to be gracious and loving but instead (often not meaning to) hurt and exiled someone like Hector. This pattern is exactly what should *not* happen in your church or mine. It definitely shouldn't happen in our personal relationships.

As you read Hector's story, were you thinking of someone you know in the LGBT community?

Maybe a good friend just confided in you that he is attracted to people of the same gender. The news caught you off guard, and now you're confused about how to respond or what to do. You know some of the things you should probably say, but you are unsure whether or not you could do it well, and if you could, when and how you should proceed.

Perhaps a daughter came out to you as a lesbian. You were shocked, horrified. You immediately became concerned about her relationship with God. There were harsh words on both sides. The rift hasn't closed to this day, but now that you've had some time to think about it, you're reminded of how much you love her, you want to know what's going on in her life, and you want to be of genuine help to her.

Or possibly you met someone at work. He's exactly the kind of person you would like to be friends with—same sense of humor, same interests, a lot of deep things to say. Also, you consider yourself an evangelistic sort of Christian, wanting to share Jesus with people who are not believers—people like this guy. But there's this one little thing: he's gay. Actually, it's not so little to you. You wonder if you can form a relationship with this person. Or would it be better to skip it and move on to find another friend?

I want to invite you to live in the tension of grace and truth. I'm not asking you to do something that you're not already doing. Christianity is filled with tension. We believe in one God, but he is Father,

Son, and Holy Spirit. Jesus was fully God and fully human. The Bible was written by human authors but inspired of God. The tension of predestination and free will has brought lively debate throughout the years. Even the whole discussion of faith and works is filled with tension. You may not have ever thought of your faith in this way, but you're already living in the tension. So when it comes to homosexuality, I want you to consider living in the tension of grace and truth. Why? Because your relationship with your family member, friend, or co-worker is totally worth it.

I hope you're ready to consider your gay friend or loved one as a whole person and to try to think about the issues of homosexuality and faith from his or her perspective. I hope you're ready to learn how to be gracious to people in the LGBT community even if it makes you nervous or unsure of the ground you're standing on. Because if you are, then you're ready to read the rest of this book.

You're about to get a glimpse of the LGBT community from the inside, to see what some think of Christians so that you can think about what kind of Christian you are going to be to them. If you're like most Christians I know, you can do better in this area.

I'm not suggesting you have been the kind of person who has actually told people in the gay community that God hates them. Quite possibly, however, at times you have been like Hector's friends. That is, you may have been un-Christlike to gay people in subtle ways—for example, acting rude or cold, making bigoted jokes or using offensive terms, imagining the worst about them, not taking them seriously, or having holier-than-thou spiritual arrogance. If so, then you're about to get some strong encouragement to make a change in your life. And beyond avoiding mistakes, you're going to learn how to have positive, Christlike interactions with people in the gay community.

As a result, I believe that you'll feel more comfortable around people in your life who identify as LGBT. You'll probably be more confident in building authentic relationships and more certain of what you believe. You'll have the joy of knowing that God is using you to love people into a relationship with him through Christ. The ultimate goal is not to get another "evangelism trophy"; rather, it is to love people the way that God has loved you. The win in all of this is showing God's love.

And by the way, the lessons you learn here aren't just for dealing with the LGBT community. With a little adapting, they can apply to your relationships with people from every sort of community or category that is different from you. I'll be referring to some of those people from time to time as we consider the tension of grace and truth.

I want to warn you ahead of time about something: whichever side of the tension you feel most comfortable with (grace or truth), there will be times during your reading of this book when you may not agree with what I say. You may find yourself agreeing whole-heartedly with one statement and then disagreeing two statements down. One chapter might be in line with everything you believe, while another chapter might frustrate you to no end. This book is messy. It may feel like a roller coaster as we ride the tension between grace and truth. But I hope you'll stick with me to the end, because I believe this book can change you—permanently.

On that Sunday when I was about to preach the "For or Against" sermon about homosexuality in front of my parents, I was living in the tension between grace and truth, between biblical theology and homosexuality, between courage and fear. This is the kind of tension we all need to accept again and again. My word of encouragement is this: we don't have to walk through such tension alone, and it *is* possible to come through it with good results for everyone involved.

It's time for Christians to think differently about the issue of homosexuality. It's time for Christians to own this issue.

To start getting messy, turn the page to chapter 2.

REFLECTION AND DISCUSSION QUESTIONS

1. Has there ever been a time when you had to share a tough truth with a friend? Describe how this happened.
2. Why do you think some Christians have had such a hard time building bridges with the LGBT community?
3. What are some things the Christian community can do to better dialogue with the LGBT community?
4. Have you ever known someone like Hector? Can you relate to him?
5. Do you have a difficult time relating with people who are different from you? Why or why not?

Saying Yes to the Mess

God has a lot of grace. He has been tremendously gracious to you and me over and over again. In ways we know and in ways we can barely guess at. Without our deserving a single bit of it.

The problem is, despite being the recipients of so much grace, most of us still don't understand much about passing on that grace to others. We want to give grace to other people only when it's easy or if we like the people we're dealing with. When they're different from us, they have problems we don't want to get mired in, or we have some reason not to think well of them, then giving grace doesn't seem like such a good idea.

I take some comfort from the fact that many of the people God used greatly in Bible times also had huge problems with the grace, forgiveness, and acceptance God has for people.

Jonah wanted Nineveh destroyed.

James and John tried to call fire down on others.

David and other leaders cried out for the deaths of their enemies.

Today we may look at these examples and chastise the people of the past who seem so ungracious.

We look at Jonah and shake our heads.

We see the disciples who didn't get it and thank God we aren't that dense.

We are pleased when we read that God reserved the right of vengeance for himself.

Yet, if we're honest, we have to admit that we're not so different from these people. Wouldn't you agree? I know I'm not different. I'm great with God having mercy on my next-door neighbor, my co-workers, celebrities I like, and more. But when it comes to people I have a problem with, it's different. And I know I'm not the only one.

The bottom line is this: when you deal with people, you'll always get messy. When you choose to love people who think and act dif-

> If we are going to understand messy grace, then we have to understand how to love people, no matter who they are.

ferently than you, the situation could get extremely messy. And yet these are the very people to whom Jesus has sent us in his name. If we are going to understand messy grace, then we have to understand how to love people, no matter who they are. We have to be willing to enter into those messy relationships. (And *we're* messy too, right?)

If there was ever anyone who understood what it felt like to be messy outsiders, it was my parents and me. By many churches' standards, my family would be too messy to let in the doors and we definitely wouldn't fit in. I'm sure Jesus was passionate about us even in those days, but a lot of his followers were passionately against us.

Let me introduce you to my parents and tell you what it was like to be raised in the LGBT community.

My Lesbian Moms

I was born in 1978 in Columbia, Missouri, where my mom and dad both taught in higher education. Like them, I was blessed by God to be on the shorter side. Believe it or not, today I'm shorter than most people and yet I am still taller than both my parents.

When I was two years old, my parents divorced. My mother moved out of the house and started making big changes in her life. She cut her hair very short and stopped dyeing it. She also started going to more and more parties. At one of these parties, Mom met a woman named Vera who was working on her PhD in counseling psychology. They fell in love and decided to move to Kansas City after Vera earned her doctorate. In Kansas City, Vera opened up a counseling practice while my mother started working at the University of Missouri–Kansas City.

As a child, I spent most of my weekends riding back and forth on I-70 between Columbia (where my dad still lived) and Kansas City (where my mom lived). My parents would meet halfway along I-70, stopping at a McDonald's in Concordia, Missouri, to hand me off. That McDonald's became a huge part of my childhood. It was there that I had many laughs with my parents, participated in family arguments, and learned to love the quarter pounder with cheese. (Don't hate—that cheeseburger is amazing!)

During my childhood, I never doubted that my parents loved me. I did feel confusion, however, because my home life didn't seem to be like what most other kids experienced. I wouldn't get invited to sleepovers because I was always being driven back and forth on the weekends. I didn't invite other kids to my house because I thought they might think it was weird that my mom was a lesbian.

I would spend summers, spring breaks, weekends, and holidays with my mom and Vera. Often I would accompany them to the events they were interested in. At a young age, I went to LGBT clubs, late-night parties, parades, campouts, and more. Mom and Vera would go to see lesbian comedians and concerts and would take me with them. Because I didn't have a lot of friends my own age when I was with them, their friends became my friends.

If there was a word to define my mom's friends, it was *fun*. These were people who loved to laugh, loved to get outrageous, loved to spend time together. They enjoyed creativity and celebration.

A part of the reason I responded so well to them must have been because I've always been such an extrovert. The more people the better, I always say.

Every Friday night was a time when we would go with Mom and Vera's friends to try out a new restaurant in Kansas City. We would also go to party after party, and there were always many people from the LGBT community at these parties. Many of them were lesbians and admired the fact that my mom and Vera were raising me in the community. They often wanted to ask me questions about being raised in the community, and I would answer them as best I could. Basically, I loved my mom, so I was good with whatever she wanted to do.

We lived all over the Kansas City area. First we lived in a condo north of the river. Then we moved down by the Plaza and the university. Finally we headed to the suburbs and bought a house with ten acres of forest. Even though we were outside the city limits at this point, it didn't stop the parties or the nightlife!

Unfortunately, I saw a lot of things at these parties that I should never have seen. I guess a kid with straight parents who was taken from party to party might have seen some inappropriate things too, but watching women making out with each other was different. This was in the 1980s (the best decade ever, by the way, for movies and music), and even the movies didn't have this kind of action in them.

One time, on the way home from a party, I asked Mom and Vera, "Why were those women kissing each other?"

They looked at each other, then Mom said, "It was just an expression of love."

"Kind of a sloppy, gross expression," I joked. I was always a jokester, but Vera didn't appreciate my comment.

My relationship with Vera was not easy. She was the opposite of my mom in many ways. She was taller and thinner than Mom. She also had fewer emotional highs or lows. Most of the time, even at a young age, I felt that I was competing with her for my mom's affection.

Vera was ten years older than my mom and had two kids who were adults. Her daughter was single, while her son was married and had two kids who were a few years shy of my age. I grew up with Vera's family, and in many ways they were my family. They would come to Mom and Vera's house for either Thanksgiving or Christmas. That was fine with me because, remember, I'm an extrovert and the more people living under one roof, the more I like it. I loved Vera's family then and still love them very much to this day.

What I struggled with the most was seeing Vera as an actual mother to me. My mom wanted me to see Vera in that way, but I just couldn't. Vera was impatient with me, partly because I didn't understand her as a lesbian the way she wanted me to. It seemed to me that Vera resented me and there was never anything I could do to make her happy. Being caught between two divorced parents was one thing; being caught between my mom and her lesbian lover was a different thing, one that was hard to handle.

The other issue I had with Vera was that she hated most men and consequently had a hard time liking me. From things she said and how she acted, it was obvious that men had hurt her in the past. She had identified as LGBT later in her life (even she admitted that), and many times I have wondered if her sexual identity was partly a response to the pain men had caused her. When I was young, I would talk about guns, robbers, fights, and other things that boys usually talk about. I could tell she was disgusted by it all. Actually, I don't think I ever measured up to her standards and expectations.

Mom and Vera were very political and about as liberal as one could get, especially in the decade of Ronald Reagan and George H. W. Bush. Both were card-carrying members of the ACLU, served on the board of directors for GLAAD in Kansas City, and went to rallies for Mondale, Dukakis, and other left-wing politicians. They educated me in liberal political views and the reasons they believed these views were better than conservative ones.

Besides introducing me to the gay and lesbian movement and politics, they desired for me to be as cultured as possible. During the summers, they would enroll me in different classes or programs to enhance my understanding of the world around me. I took writing classes at the University of Missouri–Kansas City, acting classes, art classes, and so on. (In a later chapter I'll tell a funny story about what happened in one of these summer classes.) I'll always be glad for the ways in which both Mom and Vera expanded my horizons and enriched my life.

My Gay Dad

It's more than a little symbolic that I spent the "fun" times of the year (weekends, holidays, and so on) with my mom and the "serious" part of the year (the school semesters) with my dad. While my mom and her friends were a lot of fun, my dad was much more serious. Not that we didn't have a good time together, but he worked a lot and led a quiet, almost reclusive life.

Dad taught at local colleges in Columbia, Missouri. When I was with him, I would spend much of my time downstairs watching television while he graded papers or worked on his PhD. Sometimes we would go out to a movie or for ice cream, but he was usually engaged in his academic labors upstairs in his study. There would also be seasons where my dad seemed to struggle with anger and frustration. I think my dad had anger from his childhood and definitely from the divorce. On some Sundays we would go to church, and I would find that it always helped his attitude.

We attended an Episcopal church in Columbia. To me, church was b-o-r-i-n-g! Confusing too. There were times during the service when we would kneel, other times when we would stand, still other times when we would sing, and then we would sit and eventually do everything all over again. I began to imagine that I was going through some kind of workout routine. Today I can appreciate the value in liturgical worship practices, but as a kid who didn't have things adequately explained to me, I didn't understand what it all meant. Church didn't have a big impact on my life at this time; it was just a routine my dad and I went through sometimes.

In contrast to my mother, who was very involved with the LGBT community, my dad was in the closet. I don't know what his romantic life was like, but he did not have a lifelong devoted partner like my mother did. When I was young, my dad's attitude toward my mother's coming out was bitter (which is ironic, since he was gay at the same time). To this day, I don't know if they have ever had a real conversation with each other about their relationship or their own sexuality, but both identified as LGBT when I was very young.

The interesting thing was, I did not find out that my dad was gay until I was right out of college. I still don't know how I didn't notice it when I was younger. Certain things he said and did and certain friends he had should have tipped me off. But they didn't. Maybe it's hardest to recognize truths about the people we are closest to.

When I figured out that my dad was gay, my world was rocked. I began to have my suspicions after college, and I finally sat down to ask him. He was honest about his sexuality but guarded with what he told me. I respected that, but I walked away from the conversation not knowing how to process it all. I mean, seriously, who has *two* parents who are gay? I know there are other people out there like me, but I'm sure there are few of us. Yet this was my reality.

What bothered me the most was the way that some straight people in general, and Christians in particular, treated those in the LGBT community. In school, I heard the usual sorts of gay jokes. When I was in the car with one of my parents, either Mom or Dad would sometimes turn on a Christian radio station to mock the talk shows. Whenever the topic of homosexuality came up on these shows, it hurt me to hear how the on-air speakers would speak about the LGBT community. From the perspective of these radio personalities, it seemed as if gay people were more like faceless enemies than fellow human beings.

In the next chapter I'll describe in much more depth some of the ways Christians hurt my mom. One of my goals in writing this book is to help you feel what it is like for gay men and lesbians to be the subjects of abuse by Christians. But even before I get to all of that, I'm sure it's easy enough for you to imagine how Christians could say or do things that are hateful toward the LGBT community. Maybe you've witnessed some of this abuse yourself. Maybe you have even been responsible for some of it. If so, don't let that stop you—keep reading.

Jesus Being Himself

The way that Christians treated my parents makes me think of one of my favorite stories about Jesus. It's in John, a book of the Bible that holds a special place in my heart because this gospel does such an amazing job of showing how personable Jesus was and how much he cared for people.

We see one of these caring moments in John 8. Early one morning, Jesus was in the middle of teaching a crowd of people at the temple when a peculiar thing happened to him.[3]

> The teachers of the law and the Pharisees brought in a
> woman caught in adultery. They made her stand before the
> group and said to Jesus, "Teacher, this woman was caught in
> the act of adultery. In the Law Moses commanded us to
> stone such women. Now what do you say?" They were using
> this question as a trap, in order to have a basis for accusing
> him. (verses 3–6)

The first thing we might notice about this situation is that somebody is missing. I mean, where's the dude? Did this woman's lover—the guy whose bed she just got dragged out of—get handed a Get Out of Jail Free card or something?

Only the female partner in sin was being forced to face the music. In that time and place, while promiscuous men often got a pass, women of loose morals were looked down on severely. Or to put it another way, this woman hauled before Jesus was considered to be *messy*. She was bad news, just like my family was when I was growing up. And just like gay and lesbian people are in the eyes of many Christians today.

What really makes me mad about the situation Jesus faced is that the teachers of the Law and the Pharisees were supposed to be the pastors, the people you would go to if your life was messy and you needed spiritual help. Instead of pastoring this woman, though, these religious know-it-alls took advantage of her and were ready to kill her just so they could get Jesus in trouble.

The Old Testament Law prescribed death for people guilty of adultery (see Leviticus 20:10; Deuteronomy 22:22). Was Jesus going to insist on the strict application of this command in this particular case, or would he refuse to do so — and thus discredit himself in the eyes of the more rigid people, such as these religious leaders and their fans? It seemed like a tough spot for Jesus.

His response? "Jesus bent down and started to write on the ground with his finger" (verse 6). Umm . . . okay. Not sure that I would do something like that. But one thing I notice when I read the Gospels is that everything Jesus did had a point.

Many people wonder what Jesus was writing in the dust. Some people believe he was writing down some commands from the Old Testament Law. Others suggest he was writing the sins of the religious leaders in the dust. Or maybe he was just doodling to pass the time while the religious leaders had their say. Who knows?

I can't tell you for sure what he was up to when he wrote in the dirt. But one time when I was preparing a sermon on this passage I ran across an interesting Old Testament verse that might relate to this story. Jeremiah 17:13 says,

LORD, you are the hope of Israel;
    all who forsake you will be put to shame.
Those who turn away from you will be written
       in the dust
    because they have forsaken the LORD,
    the spring of living water.

In light of this verse, I think I know the point Jesus was making here: The adulterous woman had not forsaken God. Rather, the teachers of the Law and the Pharisees had forsaken God. (So, who was really messy here?)

These legalists apparently didn't get the point quickly, because "they kept on questioning him." It went on until finally Jesus had enough. "He straightened up and said to them, 'Let any one of you who is without sin be the first to throw a stone at her'" (verse 7).

What Jesus said here is nothing short of brilliant!

Jesus, far from being trapped by the Pharisees, now had the Pharisees trapped—and not just in one way but in two. The Pharisees believed that all people are sinners. So if they picked up a rock and threw it at the woman after what Jesus said, they would be guilty of lying (that is, breaking one of the Ten Commandments), because they would be saying that they had no sin—an impossibility. Even more serious than that, they would be guilty of blasphemy. God is the only one without sin, so if they picked up a rock and threw it, in a sense they would be claiming to be God. Blasphemy, like adultery, was punishable by death. The very rocks they hurled could be picked up and thrown back at them.

Like I said, Jesus was brilliant!

He went back to writing in the dirt while it got really quiet and the implications of what he'd said filtered through the minds of his opponents. Finally someone stirred. "Those who heard began to go away one at a time, the older ones first, until only Jesus was left, with the woman still standing there" (verse 9).

It was still early, but can you imagine the day this woman had already had? Caught in the act of adultery. Grabbed by some religious leaders and hauled off to the temple. Humiliated before a bunch of the townspeople she lived among. Threatened with immediate execution. Then inexplicably spared. Makes for an eventful morning for her.

When the religious leaders wandered off, she must have been wondering what was next. What actually happened must have been the most amazing part of all:

> Jesus straightened up and asked her, "Woman, where are they? Has no one condemned you?"
>
> "No one, sir," she said.
>
> "Then neither do I condemn you," Jesus declared. "Go now and leave your life of sin." (verses 10–11)

Let's think about how this reaction illustrates Jesus's character. Two verses at the beginning of the gospel—John 1:14 and 17—say that Jesus came full of "grace and truth." When releasing the woman caught in adultery, he displayed both qualities. Jesus had grace when he set the woman free. He alone, being the true God, had every right to condemn this woman if he wanted to, but instead he chose the path of mercy and forgiveness. Yet he also had truth. He did not condone her activity. As a matter of fact, he used strong language for it: *sin*. (Now there's a word we're not supposed to throw around today!)

This story is a call for us to live in the tension of grace and truth.

I've often wondered what the best word is to describe this tension. While thinking through this story, I finally figured it out: love is the tension of grace and truth.

Here's what I mean. When you have a person in your life involved in activities or life choices that aren't healthy, you feel the tension. On the one hand, you feel extreme love for them, but on the other hand, you know that somehow you need to speak truth into their life. It's the same feeling when someone you love makes decisions outside the bounds of Scripture—you have the desire to show them grace and help them understand the truth of the matter. If you have ever been in this circumstance before, then you understand.

> Love is the tension of grace and truth.

We see Jesus's loving action toward the woman throughout the story, and it's because he was living in that tension of grace and truth. Jesus loved her enough to tell her the truth and show her grace.

Somehow, despite the messiness we encounter, we have to figure out how to be the bearers of grace *and* truth, because it always results in love.

Messy Grace

If we are going to be honest, Christians do not have the best track record in loving people. Especially, evangelical and conservative Christians don't have the best track record in loving people who are different from us. We have issues with people who have different political ideologies, different theologies, or different preferences in sexuality than we do. Sometimes we do a better job of wounding others over our differences than we do in building them up.

Part of the problem is that we get trapped in the wrong thinking. We think that we are not supposed to love people who live in a way that is contrary to what God says. Atheists, abortion doctors, legalists, alcoholics, convicts, hypocrites, the sexually immoral, gossipers, and anyone who seems to be on the opposite end of any kind of spectrum from us—these are people we are fearful to get involved with because it seems so messy.

> We get trapped in the wrong thinking. We think that we are not supposed to love people who live in a way that is contrary to what God says.

It's a good thing Jesus didn't decide that *we* were too messy to get involved with! The apostle Paul said, "God demonstrates his own love for us in this: While we were still sinners, Christ died for us" (Romans 5:8). *While we were still sinners . . .*

- *Not* when we had it all together.
- *Not* when we were moral and clean-cut and smelled good.
- *Not* when we started attending church.
- *Not* when we started acting the way Christians act.
- *Not* when we started wearing Christian T-shirts, listening to Christian music, or otherwise participating in the Christian subculture.
- *Not* when we started believing.

Paul said that *while we were still sinners,* God extended an offer of relationship toward us!

We need to express that same kind of love—a love that doesn't wait for people to be perfect or get everything in order before beginning a friendship with us. It's imperative that we have grace for people while they are still thinking, speaking, and acting in ways we might not agree with. And we need to overcome our own inner resistance to getting involved in a relationship with them. A real mark of spiritual maturity is *how* we treat someone who is different from us.

People in the LGBT community aren't a faceless enemy. They are real people who need to know that God loves them. People like my dad, my mom, and Vera. People like some of the other gay men and lesbians I'll be introducing to you in the rest of the book.

> People in the LGBT community aren't a faceless enemy. They are real people who need to know that God loves them.

Their lives are far from perfect, sure. Just like ours. But unless we choose to get involved in their lives in a loving way, they may never know the Lord who loves them.

To see this connection, let's turn our attention to 1 John 4:7–11:

> Dear friends, let us love one another, for love comes from God. Everyone who loves has been born of God and knows God. Whoever does not love does not know God, because God is love. This is how God showed his love among us: He sent his one and only Son into the world that we might live through him. This is love: not that we loved God, but that he loved us and sent his Son as an atoning sacrifice for our sins. Dear friends, since God so loved us, we also ought to love one another.

John gets harsh in this passage and says that if we don't love other people, then we don't really know who God is. It seems strange, but it's true: a lot of people are sitting in church every single weekend thinking they are growing in their faith, yet they are weak because they are judging others and refusing to engage the people God wants them to.

Let me say this in another way: God paid a hefty price when he allowed his Son to be sent into the world to be tortured and killed. What does it say about our opinion of the cross, then, if we are not willing to go and tell people about the death Jesus died for them— just because we don't agree with them or they make us feel uncomfortable? What does it say about our opinion of the blood of Christ if we are willing to let it go to waste by not bragging on what God has done to save those who are lost?

If I were God and I watched my Son die on the cross for the sins of the world, and the very people for whom he died refused to share that message with other people he died for, I would be pretty upset. Wouldn't you?

In that light, I don't think God is worried about our getting messy or feeling uncomfortable.

Blood, Blood Everywhere

The first recorded comment by Jesus about what he had in mind for his followers comes in Mark 1:17. The Lord said to the fishermen-brothers Simon and Andrew, "Come, follow me, and I will send you out to fish for people."

Fishing for people. Sounds rather charming, doesn't it? Even relaxing. What could be so bad about netting souls for Jesus? Fishing is a neat, clean pastime, right?

Ha!

Growing up in Missouri, I sometimes went fishing on a lake with some of my extended family and friends. I always had a great time going fishing in the boat. It seemed to be all fun and no fuss—

sit around with people I enjoyed, talk, bask in the weather, reel in a fish occasionally. What's not to like?

Then one day I caught a fish and happened to mention somebody else cleaning it for me. I don't remember how old I was, but apparently I was judged to be old enough to start taking more responsibility as a fisherman. "You catch it, you clean it," proclaimed a relative in the boat.

Really? I've got to clean this thing?

I had never cleaned a fish before, but I had seen it done and so I started to get cocky about it. I began to think cleaning my fish would be easy.

It was not easy. Not easy at all.

I don't know if the knife was dull or if I was just really unskillful at wielding it, but what ensued in our kitchen later that day was one ugly sight. It could have been staged for a B slasher film. By the end of the process, blood was all over the sink, blood was all over me, blood was on the floor. What was left of the carcass looked nothing like a fish. We cooked it and it was a great dinner, but boy, I got messy beforehand. There was no way around it.

> The grace of God is bigger than any of us is willing to admit.

You know where I'm going with this: if Jesus calls us to be fishers of people and to get involved in the lives of others, we're going to get messy.

Why? *Because the grace of God is bigger than any of us is willing to admit.*

People are messy.

Sacrifice is messy.

Talking about important issues is messy.

Helping others is messy.

Love is messy.

And that's all right. We can pursue people for Christ anyway.

In the next chapter, I'm going to tell you how to pursue relationships with the LGBT people in your life and how not to.

REFLECTION AND DISCUSSION QUESTIONS

1. Has there ever been a time when you were shown grace, meaning you didn't deserve the positive treatment you got? What was that like?

2. In John 8, Jesus has the same grace for the Pharisees that he does for the woman caught in adultery. Why is this?

3. How do you see grace and truth in this statement by Jesus in John 8:11: "Neither do I condemn you. Go now and leave your life of sin."

4. How and why is the grace of God so messy?

5. Name one person you need to reach out to and share God's messy grace. Why does this person need the grace of God?

3

The Right Kind of Pursuit

It was a Saturday morning the summer I was nine. Mom and Vera woke me up early to tell me that we were going to march in a parade.

"What kind of a parade?" I asked.

"A gay pride parade," Vera responded.

"You get to march with us and stand up for our rights," my mom encouraged.

This parade, starting near the Plaza and continuing on to an area of Kansas City called Westport, would be the first gay pride parade I would ever march in, though it would not be the last. It was also one of the earliest times when I saw some self-proclaimed Christians pursue my mom's community. Unfortunately, they pursued the community in a way that could do nothing but bring harm.

The descriptions of abuse I'm going to give you in this chapter may seem extreme to you. They may seem (and I hope they are) outliers in the way that professed Christians treat the LGBT community. It would be easy for us to write them off as extremists, but we need to pay attention.

As you read the story that is to come, ask yourself if there are some ways—perhaps not so extreme—that you have contributed to the

mistreatment of people in "alternative lifestyles." Have you used de-
rogatory language to refer to gay people or their sexual preferences?
Have you posted unkind messages or insulting cartoons about the
LGBT community on social media? Have you told demeaning jokes?
Have you cold-shouldered a gay person at work? Have you let a gay
couple in your neighborhood know you would prefer it if they would
move on? Have you told a gay joke and insulted someone who was gay?
Have you pointedly avoided shaking hands with someone who is gay?

If any of these things ring
true to you, I can assure you that
you're not alone. You're probably
already sorry and want to know
how to do better.

In that case, I have some
helpful things to say to you in this

> We should be pursuing
> relationships with
> members of the LGBT
> community the same
> way God pursues us.

chapter and the ones to follow. The first point is simple but founda-
tional: we should be pursuing relationships with members of the
LGBT community the same way God pursues us.

In love, not hate.

"Christians Hate Gay People"

The gay pride parade was a circus. I don't mean that as an insult
whatsoever. I mean that it literally (to me as a young kid) looked like
a circus. There were clowns, bright colors, people dancing, and floats.
Shouting, laughter, and music filled the air. People were wearing
clothes the likes of which I had never seen before. Some were hardly
wearing anything at all. Some people were imitating sexual acts on
floats.

There was really no rhyme or reason to how the parade was

organized. Hundreds of people just showed up to march. Even more people began lining the streets. The band started playing loudly, sounding just like a high school marching band. Vera laughed and my mom let out a cheer. We were off!

Along the route, someone (I'm not sure who) placed a sign in my hands that compared angry preachers to the Nazis. The sign I carried was hugely popular. Many gave me a thumbs-up and agreed with me as I walked down the street.

The streets were lined with thousands of people cheering us on. Some jumped in the parade and started walking with us. By the time we got to the end of the parade route, we had more people with us than we had when we started. Looking back on it, I'm reminded of that scene from *Rocky II* where the boxer starts running down the street, a few people start running after him, and by the time he gets to those famous steps and runs up them, hundreds are with him.

I can honestly say that the parade was a fun time.

The fun, however, didn't last.

At the end of the parade we encountered a group of Christians holding up signs that said things like this:

"Fags go away."

"Jesus has no room for you."

"You'll burn in hell."

They were only a few people, and to this day I am not sure which church they were from, but they were vocal and antagonistic.

Some of the members of the parade tried to go over to them and talk to them about their signs, but the hecklers greeted them with water guns and hoses. One of the guys from the parade yelled, "They're spraying urine all over us!" It was an ugly scene.

One woman from the parade started crying and yelled at the critics, "Why do you hate us so much?"

No dialogue happened that day. Just more finger-pointing and yelling.

I looked at my mom and Vera. They were frozen in one spot, staring at what was going on and shaking their heads in disbelief. I asked my mom, "Why are those people acting like that?"

She replied sharply, "Well, Caleb, they're Christians, and Christians hate gay people. Christians don't like anyone who's not like them."

Anger and bitterness started welling up in my young heart. I could not believe the way my friends from the parade were being treated. The church I attended infrequently with my father wasn't big on using the Bible, but I knew enough about Jesus to know that he would not act like that. I knew that I never wanted to be a Christian.

I started yelling at the group of "Christians" who were spraying everyone. My mother immediately stood in front of me (I think to protect me from being sprayed) and told me not to engage them. I didn't care. A sense of injustice was playing out in my heart.

Mom and Vera hauled me from there to the place where dinner was waiting for everyone who had marched in the parade. They seemed to be able to move on from what had just happened and began greeting their friends. Me? I couldn't move on. My mind was stuck on the awful way those "Jesus followers" had acted.

It wouldn't be my last time facing people like this.

More Trouble

My mom was loud and proud about her identity as a lesbian. The back end of her purple RAV4, in addition to being plastered with political bumper stickers, displayed stickers that said things like "Graduate of Thelma and Louise finishing school," "I must sprinkle you with fairy dust," and "Lorena Bobbitt for surgeon general." (I think the last bumper sticker was the funniest.) You can imagine that when I got my license and started driving Mom's car, I got some weird looks.

Not long after the parade, my mother and I were visiting some family in Topeka, Kansas. We went there often, as my cousins, aunt, uncle, and grandma lived there. One day Mom and I were driving down a street in Topeka and pulled up to a stoplight. As I looked to my right, I saw a lot of people on the street corner holding up signs that looked familiar. I'm not sure if it was the same group of people who had protested the parade I had marched in earlier or not, but nonetheless it was a group of angry Christians. This time they saw my mother's bumper stickers and started pointing and laughing at her. I heard profanity and four-letter words hurled at my mother.

I looked over at my mom. She wasn't saying anything. She was just looking forward, and a single tear rolled down her cheek.

"Why do they have to be so mean?" I asked.

Even though I was just a little kid, I was protective of my mother. I made a decision that seemed appropriate at the time. I rolled down my window, stuck my body halfway out, and gave the sign wavers my middle finger. Not my finest moment.

My mom didn't try to stop me, but the light turned green and we started driving away. I sat back down in the car and rolled up the window. Then I looked at my mom and asked, "Are you going to be okay?"

She just smiled at me and said, "Don't worry, I'll be okay. I'm just glad I'm not like those people who are so controlled by their hate."

Staring out the window, I didn't understand why people had to be so ugly. What had my mother done wrong? What had she ever done to those people to make them hate her so much? Why were they so against her when they didn't even know her?

That was not okay with me, and I know now that it wasn't okay with God either.

The Life of the Party

I seriously doubt Jesus would have been one of the people holding signs on the side of the street. He was the opposite. The more you read the Gospels, the more you see that Jesus was strategic about pursuing those others wouldn't.

Even when Jesus had just started his ministry, he was already being criticized. He spent too much time with people the religious leaders were uncomfortable with. He loved the sick, healed lepers, hung out with prostitutes, and interacted with Roman soldiers. One of the biggest offenses was in how he treated tax collectors.

In Jesus's day, many of the religious leaders and other Jews hated tax collectors more than almost everybody else. Some of those tax collectors were Jewish people who were working for the Romans, the occupying power of the day. Those tax collectors got away with over-charging the people and pocketing the difference. In other words, they were both sellouts and crooks. I can easily imagine that people shunned them, shot dirty looks at them, and shouted epithets at them. If there had been a Tax Collectors' Pride Parade, the curbs would have been lined with people carrying angry signs and urine-filled water guns.

Yet Jesus had a different way of interacting with people from this hated group.

The story begins like this: "As Jesus went on from there, he saw a man named Matthew sitting at the tax collector's booth. 'Follow me,' he told him, and Matthew got up and followed him" (Matthew 9:9). Where was Jesus headed with Matthew? Not to some quiet place where he could berate the tax collector out of the hearing of Roman soldiers. No, they were going to Matthew's house for a dinner party!

This is the kind of stuff that makes me love Jesus. He just didn't care about what other people thought of his actions. He didn't care what the Romans thought. He didn't care what the Jewish people thought. He didn't care what the religious leaders thought. He didn't even care what his disciples thought. His concern was doing the will of God and loving the lost so they could become worshipers of God and bring him glory.

I've even wondered if Jesus got himself a dinner invite with Matthew in order to set up a fight with the Pharisees. Think about it. Matthew was a tax collector and probably a wealthy man. In a culture where most people had one-room houses, Matthew's house probably had multiple rooms and a patio. No doubt this party, with Jesus's popularity and Matthew's friends, meant a packed house. I'm sure the partygoers spilled out onto the streets. Jesus knew that the Pharisees and other people would see him and his disciples there and raise an issue with it.

Whether that was Jesus's plan or not, it's exactly what happened. "While Jesus was having dinner at Matthew's house, many tax collectors and sinners came and ate with him and his disciples. When the Pharisees saw this, they asked his disciples, 'Why does your teacher eat with tax collectors and sinners?'" (verses 10–11).

If we know anything about Pharisees, we're not surprised they acted like this. Honestly, though, there's something about the disciples here that bothers me.

The Pharisees would never even think about going into Matthew's house and being associated with "those people." They would definitely be on the outskirts of the party. Yet who did they get close enough to talk to? The disciples!

The disciples must have been on the outskirts of the party too. This tells me there's a good chance that at least some of the disciples were as worried about being associated with these people as the Pharisees were.

Jesus was different. He was probably in the center of everything and talking with people. Again, he didn't care what other people thought. He was more concerned about loving others than he was about anyone's opinion. So he decided to teach both the Pharisees and the disciples a huge lesson.

Jesus overheard what the Pharisees said to the disciples. Perhaps Jesus saw the Pharisees and disciples talking and went over to them, or maybe he was wandering around the party. In any case, Jesus said, "It is not the healthy who need a doctor, but the sick. But go and learn what this means: 'I desire mercy, not sacrifice.' For I have not come to call the righteous, but sinners" (verses 12–13).

The religious folk, such as the Pharisees, were already righteous (or they *thought* they were). So Jesus's place was not with them but with those who needed him and welcomed him. He wanted to do spiritual work among the tax collectors and other shady characters gathered for the house party. He didn't care if others didn't like his choice to spend time with these people.

Those in attendance at the party also learned a lesson. They were the outcast and the downcast—the fringe of society. They were used to being passed by in the streets and not being invited anywhere nice. Yet now they learned that God was chasing after them. God was aware of them. God loved them. As helpless as they were in their spiritual state, God was there to guide them into a better life.

When I think about this story, I think of the word *pursuit*. Jesus was pursuing people whose lives were messy and whose hearts were far from God but who were open to hearing about him. So Jesus went to a place where no religious leader was willing to go. He built a relationship with people no religious leader wanted to build a relationship with. He brought his disciples into a group that no religious leader would want to be associated with.

Jesus saw these people and pursued them, meeting them where they were. In the same way, God pursues us and meets us where we are.

Pursuing Like God Does

Our God is a God who has always pursued people, regardless of how far away from him they may have seemed. From Israel to us, God still loves and pursues. Scripture proves this over and over again. Here are a few examples:

> Surely your goodness and love will follow me
>   all the days of my life. (Psalm 23:6)

> The Son of Man came to seek and to save the lost. (Luke 19:10)

> No one can come to me unless the Father who sent me draws them. (John 6:44)

Notice that the last two examples come from the Gospels, from Jesus's life.

Jesus pursued people in both grace and truth. There were times when he was extremely loving, and there were times when he was loving but still had to tell the harsh truth.

We, too, need to tell people the truth. It may not be what they want to hear. But we certainly don't have to do it with the cruel harshness of the people who jeered at my mom and Vera from the street corners.

Now, there may be times, seasons, and places where street evangelism is the best way to go. John the Baptist, Jesus, Paul, Peter, and many others were street preachers, in a sense. God blessed their words, and I believe that God blesses the words of street preachers today, even if they are words that are hard to accept. But their message should have a completely different tone from the one used by the parade hecklers.

Usually it's better to share hard truths with people in the context of a relationship you have already formed. If we know their past, their hurts and pains, we can share the truth in a nonjudgmental way. This is how God pursues us with the truth. God is near us through all the days of our lives, pursuing us with the truth in love until we turn to him.

> God is near us through all the days of our lives, pursuing us with the truth in love until we turn to him.

I believe that in the party Jesus attended with Matthew, even though he was loving toward the party attendees, there would have come a time in a personal relationship where he would have shared hard truth. The New Testament offers multiple examples of Jesus sharing the truth in love. Part of the pursuit is being honest with people, but doing it in a loving way.

In God, we have the best model and mentor in pursuing others. We should pursue others like our loving heavenly Father pursues us, his children. This is a lesson I can understand better now, after having become a father myself.

How a Father Pursues

My wife and I wanted to have kids as soon as we got married. But for a long time we just couldn't get pregnant. We went to doctors, prayed, and bought books on the subject. After a couple of years, it got pretty depressing. I dealt with my depression by jumping deeper into work and secluding myself. My wife dealt with her depression in a more destructive manner: by watching Hugh Grant movies. We would sit on the couch together and watch movies in which the main character would finally have a baby, and my wife would immediately start crying.

In such a moment, I discovered, you have two options: reclaim your manhood from Hugh Grant or get your wife pregnant. I chose the latter of the two.

We went to a fertility clinic for help, and afterward my wife got pregnant with our son. We couldn't believe it! Amy and I celebrated by going to Babies "R" Us and trying out every maternity chair we could find. We must have spent four hours in that store. We were there so long the employees started offering us refreshments.

Not only that, but we became the annoying couple you wouldn't want to invite over. I mean, if you invited the Kaltenbachs to your house, you needed to be prepared for a long evening of talking about their pregnancy. We didn't care that people found us boring; we were so excited to be pregnant that we told everyone.

We also watched movies that romanticized pregnancy and labor. I remember one movie in particular where the child came out clean and happy, a light shone down from heaven, he grabbed the dad's finger, and they locked eyes. I just knew that my first moment with my child would be like that.

Hardly.

Everything was great until the pain started. My wife then became someone different from the person I had married. I went over to comfort her during the hard contractions, and she glared at me and said, "Don't you touch me right now!"

I backed away and said, "Okay, Emily Rose, Linda Blair, whoever you are."

A nurse started the drugs and Amy's pain went away. She immediately started loving God and others again.

Several hours later, it was time for the child to make his entrance into the world. When the doctor showed up, she put on what looked like a welding mask and armor. The nurses were putting on masks and armor as well.

I went up to the doctor and asked, "Is something going to explode?"

She laughed and said no. Then she told me to wait in the corner.

My wife started pushing and pushing and pushing for what seemed to be forever. I was waiting for the moment when my son would come out and I would catch him as he slipped into our world.

When my son was finally born, I felt like I was in a Sigourney Weaver space alien movie. His body was a color I had never seen before—I don't even think they have a crayon that represents that color. He made the most awful noise I have ever heard in my life. He smelled very . . . different, to put it mildly. He was so slimy that I could barely hold on to him.

The nurse asked me what I thought.

I said, "He looks like a turtle!"

But let me be serious about something. When I held my son for the first time, I felt an attachment and a love like I'd never had before. A few years later, when I held my daughter for the first time— same thing. It was instantaneous! When I first held my kids, in that moment I would have done anything for them. I just loved them so much and knew there was nothing they could do to make me unlove them.

Ever since I held my kids for the first time, I've been pursuing my kids, in order to stay connected to them.

I am not a perfect father. I don't always make the best decisions. Sometimes I lose my cool. But one thing I do right is that I pursue my son and daughter with my love and pursue them for God so that they'll know his love. No matter who they become or what they do in their lives, it will never stop me from loving them or pursuing them.

> When you're criticized for the things Jesus was, you know you're doing something right. If you're not criticized, then maybe it's time to reexamine what you're doing.

That is the same way our heavenly Father feels about everybody! He pursues us with his love no matter how we mess up.

And he expects us to pursue other people in the same way. So we should never be the ones who hold up hateful signs on street corners, post offensive messages on social media, or belittle others because of their beliefs. We should be people who share the truth in love, because it is the best representation of how God chases after us.

Spend time with people who are different from you.

Befriend people who have different political beliefs.

Go out to lunch with people who have different values than you.

Invite people from different religious backgrounds to your house for dinner.

Go to parties attended by gay men and lesbians who don't believe in God.

In other words, get out of your comfort zone and pursue others.

Here's the truth: if you chase after people like Jesus did, you *will* be criticized—by some Christians, no less. But I've heard others say (and I agree with it), "If I'm going to be criticized for anything, I'd rather be criticized for the things that Jesus was." When you're criticized for the things Jesus was, you know you're doing something right. If you're not criticized, then maybe it's time to reexamine what you're doing.

It's time to pursue others.

Bring on the critics!

REFLECTION AND DISCUSSION QUESTIONS

1. How do you think members of the LGBT community feel when they see self-identified Christians holding up signs on street corners and hear the derogatory remarks such people make? What picture of Jesus does that paint to them?

2. How does Matthew 9:9–13 show what kinds of people are important to Jesus? Why were the Pharisees so offended that Jesus attended this party?

3. Look at some of the Scripture passages in this chapter. What do they say about God's pursuit of people? What people does God pursue?

4. How can you pursue people with the same passion that God does? What can you do to spend time with people who are different from you?

5. When was the last time you were criticized for something Jesus was criticized for? What happened?

Us Versus Them?

You know what drives me crazy? The names we call people who disagree with our Christian values or those who are different from us. Names like:

- They
- Them
- Those
- The others
- Those people
- The other side

I hate those names. I've heard different Christians refer to my parents and other people in the gay community with terms like these more times than I can remember. Yet when we refer to people by terms that keep them at a distance, it shows we have lost our understanding of the gospel and God's desire for people.

If we're going to enter into a relationship of messy grace with our gay friends and family (or anybody else who's distinctly different from us), we need a change of mind. We need to stop thinking of "them" as the enemy. "They're" not the enemy. "They're" not even all that different from us. We shouldn't be putting up barriers or maintaining a safe distance from "them."

We need to lose our us-versus-them mentality. We're all sinners in need of Jesus.

Sometimes the young are better at understanding this than adults.

The Note

The summer after I participated in my first gay pride parade (the story told in the previous chapter), my mom enrolled me in a young writers class at the University of Missouri–Kansas City. The class had about fifteen students in it. Each day we would gather in a university classroom with our teacher and do writing exercises together. We also began working on our final projects. For my project, I embarked on a short story about a werewolf in a small town. I'm pretty sure I ripped off Stephen King, but who knows, maybe one day it will get published.

What I remember most from the class is the girl who sat next to me: Angela. She was gorgeous! She had long hair, was tall, had dark brown eyes, smiled a lot, and looked like a young version of Whitney Houston. We struck up a friendship during the class. Truth be told, I thought she dug my chili. I was not used to girls talking to me much, so this was huge for me.

One day after lunch I walked to my desk, and there was a note for me in Angela's handwriting. *Yes!* I thought. Finally she had given in to her fleshly desires! The note was folded in half, and on the front she'd drawn a heart with an arrow through it. I mean, could there be any clearer sign that something amazing was about to happen between us? All the conversations we'd had, and all those boring stories about her cat that I'd pretended to listen to, were about to pay off.

I eagerly opened the note, only to find . . .

A gospel presentation.

What? Come on, seriously?

I was expecting gushing sentences about how she felt about me. Instead, she'd written a letter explaining to me how Jesus had died on the cross for my sins and how she wanted me to be in heaven with her. My heart sank.

It wasn't just my romantic disappointment that made me upset. I thought what she said in her letter was nonsense. To me, Christians were people who thought my mom was wrong, and I wanted nothing to do with them.

A few minutes later, Angela came up to me and asked if I had gotten the note.

I said yes and, smiling, assured her I would think about what she'd written. Then I gave her a hug. (At least I got a hug out of it.) Inside I was thinking, *No way.*

Angela and I finished the class and lost contact. I moved on.

Looking back now, though, I realize this girl was the first Christian I knew who didn't look at me or my family as if we were the enemy. I had told her about my parents, and she didn't care. She didn't think people in my parents' community were out to get her. She simply knew she had to let me know how Jesus really felt about me. She was willing to engage those who were far away from God, and she saw them as important.

Jesus for Everyone

Angela was representing Jesus better than many Christians do. Jesus is someone who meets people where they are and doesn't mind getting involved in their messy lives. And that's when things start to change.

You see, he's a healer. He heals physical and spiritual ills. Most people in his day tried to avoid the sick, but not Jesus. Consider what Jesus did after preaching at a small-town synagogue one Sabbath day: "As soon as they left the synagogue, they went with James and John to the home of Simon and Andrew. Simon's mother-in-law was in bed with a fever, and they immediately told Jesus about her. So he went to her, took her hand and helped her up. The fever left her and she began to wait on them" (Mark 1:29–31).

Several people deserve kudos here. First of all, Peter, because he actually wanted his mother-in-law to get better! I have a wonderful mother-in-law myself, but I have friends who, if their mothers-in-law were sick, would urge them to "head toward the light."

And then there's the mother-in-law herself. When I'm sick, I lie in bed and complain. My wife gives me a couple of days to get better before she starts getting annoyed with me. After Jesus healed Peter's mother-in-law, however, she immediately got up and started taking care of him.

But Jesus himself, of course, deserves the most praise. He had compassion and used his miracle power of healing for a woman in need.

Well, it didn't take long for the word to get out that a healer was in town. As soon as the day came to an end at sundown and the people were relieved of their Sabbath travel restrictions, they started flocking to Jesus from all around. So after healing Peter's mother-in-law, Jesus spent his evening healing others, both physically and spiritually.

The gospel of Mark tells us, "That evening after sunset the people brought to Jesus all the sick and demon-possessed. The whole town gathered at the door, and Jesus healed many who had various diseases. He also drove out many demons, but he would not let the demons speak because they knew who he was" (1:32–34).

Keep in mind, these were people who were not being ministered to by the strict Pharisees and priests. They were the outcasts and downtrodden of society. Yet Jesus—God incarnate—spent the night with them, healing and casting out demons. I can only imagine that the hours he spent healing the people were physically exhausting and tough for him.

You know what I bet the best reward was for Jesus? What he saw afterward. As people went home, the street was littered with objects: crutches, casts, bandages, chains, dirty clothing, walking sticks.

The streets were filled with objects that at one time had aided the sick and possessed. The streets were filled with objects they no longer needed because of Jesus's healing and presence with them.

I'm sure, during the course of Jesus's ministry, there were times when he had to pass by a lot of people who were sick. Not this night. This night he was able to make a difference.

Jesus saw these people as wounded, not a burden.

Jesus saw these people as hurting, not in the way.

Jesus saw these people as an opportunity, not a liability.

Jesus saw these people as God's children, not sinners who got what they deserved.

Jesus saw these people as testimonies of the gospel, not moochers of religion.

Jesus was for them, not against them.

Can the same be said about us?

A Change of Mentality

Living in California in 2008 was a tense time. Why?

Prop 8.

In November 2008, Barack Obama was elected president. Proposition 8 was also passed in California. This proposition defined marriage as being between one man and one woman. Earlier, the California Supreme Court had overturned Proposition 22, which had also defined marriage as being between a man and a woman. The response from many to the overturning was to create a new proposition that would renew Prop 22. Not many in California expected Prop 8 to pass, but it did.

Why was it so tense living in California during that time?

On the one hand, many people felt strongly about giving people the freedom to marry whomever they wanted. Some in the LGBT community were extremely vocal and political in standing up for their right to marry.[4]

On the other hand, many Christians and conservatives stood up for defining marriage as only between a man and a woman. This meant there was a definite chance of wounding people who were part of the LGBT community.

Saying it was tense is an understatement.

Now, some Christians are completely against mingling faith and politics. I'm not necessarily opposed to it. After all, the Bible says God sent many of his messengers to kings and governmental authorities. God also put his people in positions of power—people such as Joseph, Esther, Daniel, and others.

At the same time, it is delicate because of how people on each side of the aisle view each other. Conservative Christians view their involvement in politics not as an attack on people but as standing for truth. People in the LGBT community see conservatives' involvement in politics as trying to limit their rights.

I would even go so far as to say that some saw Prop 8 as downright hateful. Those against Prop 8 launched the NOH8 ("No

Hate") campaign, in which same-sex-parent families posed with duct tape on their mouths or wrote "No H8" on their faces.

One day I went on a radio show, giving my testimony about growing up in an LGBT family and finding Christ. The next day, when I walked out to my car, I saw that someone had written profanities all over my car. Obviously, the perpetrator had listened to the show.

When Prop 8 passed, there were many protests.

During this season in Southern California, an unfortunate attitude of "us versus them" prevailed. I'm not saying that either side consciously viewed the situation that way, but the attitude was there. It was personal to both sides.

> When we as Christians have an us-versus-them mentality, it creates a mind-set that one side is right and "those people" on the other side are our enemies.

When we as Christians have an us-versus-them mentality, it creates a mind-set that one side is right and "those people" on the other side are our enemies. Whether we're dealing with the LGBT community, Planned Parenthood, or any other group with values that concern us, the us-versus-them attitude takes away from our witness. It creates an illusion that these people whom Jesus died for are an enemy we need to fight.

I understand that some Christians think people in the LGBT community are out to get them. Even if that is true, our Lord says a lot about dealing with those who are against us. I love what Jesus said in Matthew 5:39–42: "If anyone slaps you on the right cheek, turn to them the other cheek also. And if anyone wants to sue you and take your shirt, hand over your coat as well. If anyone forces you to go one mile, go with them two miles. Give to the one who asks you, and do not turn away from the one who wants to borrow from you."

Jesus's comments were topical for his day and even kind of funny. In a society where people typically wore only two garments, giving up both of them would have left people naked (or close to it). Jesus was saying that if you have to go to the point of being naked for the sake of peace, then do so! Not only that, but most people in those days didn't have extensive wardrobes. Giving up both a shirt and a coat was a major sacrifice, yet Jesus said that we are to go to such lengths to love our enemies.

Jesus continued by saying that we should go two miles for the person who forces us to go one mile. In his day, the Roman soldiers could force a person to carry their heavy bag a mile so they could rest. This made Jewish people angry. I mean, would you want to carry the bag of a person who had helped to conquer your land and kill your people? Yet Jesus again amazed the crowd when he basically said, "You know those soldiers you hate so much? You know how they can force you to carry their pack for a mile? Well, I want you to go *two* miles."

Jesus summed up this part of his message by saying, "You have heard that it was said, 'Love your neighbor and hate your enemy.' But I tell you, love your enemies and pray for those who persecute you, that you may be children of your Father in heaven" (5:43–45).

Love your enemies and pray for your persecutors. That must have been shocking! Remember that Jesus's listeners were actually in danger of losing their lives to the Romans. It's a shocking principle still today.

Let's ask ourselves this: As Western Christians, what do we have to complain about? No one has conquered our country. No army is killing our people. No foreign king is reigning over us. No physical persecution is befalling us.

I do understand that while we don't have physical persecution, there is a sense in which religious liberty is being challenged more and more. In the news recently we've all heard of bakeries being sued for religious beliefs (and having it labeled as discrimination), military chaplains being cornered about their views on sexuality, and more. I think we can expect more of the same. Yet this kind of opposition is nothing new.

> The gospel isn't about who God is against. It's about who God is for.

Evangelical and conservative Christians get bent out of shape at the "liberal media." We get upset because of the names we're called. We get frustrated when people don't agree with our views. I don't understand why this is so. From the days of Paul, the principles of the gospel have always stood in stark contrast to culture. This is something we have to expect in our culture.

Some say that our country was a Christian nation once. I believe it was founded on Judeo-Christian values, but the days when we can presume that the majority in our nation share those values are passing by quickly, if they are not already gone.

I believe strongly in standing up for and teaching Christ-centered values. Those of us who follow Jesus should do that, and I'm going to talk about that later in the book. However, it seems that while many of us are teaching Christ-centered values, we are quick to turn our backs on those who disagree with us.

If Jesus called the people of his day to love and be kind to an army that literally could kill them, how much more should we have a loving attitude toward people today?

The gospel isn't about who God is against. It's about who God is for.

Not the Enemy, the Mission

Maybe it's time that we Christians focus on building bridges with the LGBT community rather than burning them. That shouldn't be as hard as it might seem. Did you know there are actually several traits that the LGBT community and Christian community have in common? Here are some of them:

- creative
- a love for people
- a strong sense for justice
- strongly committed to their cause
- staging events focused upon their cause
- vocal about defending what they believe
- intentional about sharing views with others
- committed to community and doing life together
- unashamed to be recognized for what they believe in
- passionate about wanting others to see where they're coming from
- joining groups that help them better understand what and why they believe
- developing their own resources around their community: books, movies, music, and so on

I bet you didn't know you had that much in common with the LGBT community!

Maybe it's time we seek to understand where "they" are coming from and what we might have in common with "them." As much as the LGBT community is on a mission to help you understand their views, you are on a mission to share the gospel with people of that community (as you are with people from any other community).

Let me go a step further: I think that within the mission of sharing the gospel with people in the LGBT community, we also should
recognize how much some in the Christian community have hurt
their community. We have to acknowledge that even if we aren't the
ones holding signs on street corners, we are still associated with people who have done so. I truly believe that part of sharing the gospel is
apologizing for the attitudes and actions of some Christians.

Please get this: People are not the enemy. *They are the mission.*
When I say that people are the mission, I'm not saying they are objects or pet projects. Rather, we need to value people and let them
know how much God loves them. No matter what kinds of people
you are talking about, regardless of anything (gender, ethnicity, sexuality, work, and so forth), people are always the mission. We need
to figure out how to find connecting links with them.

Look at what Paul said to some philosophers in Athens: "People
of Athens! I see that in every way you are very religious. For as I
walked around and looked carefully at your objects of worship, I
even found an altar with this inscription: TO AN UNKNOWN GOD.
So you are ignorant of the very thing you worship—and this is what
I am going to proclaim to you" (Acts 17:22–23).

Paul went out of his way to use something from Greek culture
to explain the gospel to those Athenians. He could have stuck to his
own Jewish understanding and never met them on their own turf,
but he cared enough about them to study their culture and draw
from it to show Jesus to them.

Paul could easily have said to the philosophers in Athens, "You're
just against God and don't understand the truth. You've turned your
back on him and you'll get yours." He didn't. He could have said,
"I'm just going to spend my time around people who agree with what
I agree with and have the same views I do." He didn't. Imagine if

Paul had said, "Pagans and other people are my enemy because they don't believe what I do. I'm going to do everything I can to show them that I'm right and they're wrong." But Paul went out of his way to be careful and thoughtful so he could share the gospel. He opened up about this style of evangelism in 1 Corinthians 9:19–23:

> Though I am free and belong to no one, I have made myself a slave to everyone, to win as many as possible. To the Jews I became like a Jew, to win the Jews. To those under the law I became like one under the law (though I myself am not under the law), so as to win those under the law. To those not having the law I became like one not having the law (though I am not free from God's law but am under Christ's law), so as to win those not having the law. To the weak I became weak, to win the weak. I have become all things to all people so that by all possible means I might save some. I do all this for the sake of the gospel, that I may share in its blessings.

Paul was willing to go outside his comfort zone to share the gospel with all people. He became a student of their culture and ways so he could tell them about the one who died and rose from the dead for them.

We should do the same.

I have to strain to remember someone sharing the gospel with my parents. Most of the time Christians were protesting the LGBT community and telling them Jesus was against them. I seriously can remember only one or two Christians my mom mentioned who were involved in her life in a positive way. I don't know if they were actively sharing the gospel with her, but I think they must have been or else my mom would never have mentioned them.

Remember that young girl, Angela, in my writing class who wrote me that note? When I finally did become a Christian, I thought of the note she wrote to me. It probably took a lot of courage for her to write a note like that at such a young age. She planted some seeds that took a while to grow, but they finally sprouted. I think of her from time to time and can't wait to reminisce with her in heaven.

I'm honored that I was her mission on that day.

I'm glad she had the determination to let me know that God was for me, not against me.

REFLECTION AND DISCUSSION QUESTIONS

1. Can you remember a time when someone first shared the gospel with you? What happened?

2. On the day recorded in Mark 1, why did Jesus spend so much time healing all of the people? What made the healings worth it?

3. Why do some Christians have an us-versus-them mentality with people in the LGBT community . . . or with people who don't agree with them on other issues? What can we do to stop this mentality?

4. This chapter lists some similarities that the Christian community and the LGBT community share. How might we use these similarities to relate with each other?

5. Read 1 Corinthians 9:19–23 again. What was Paul's method of evangelism? How can we apply this passage to our lives today?

The Power of Touch

For some Christians, it seems safer, easier, and certainly more pleasant to avoid the LGBT conversation than to engage in it. Some Christians choose not to think critically about it and may even avoid people in the gay community. You might be able to relate.

Maybe at the coffee shop you frequent, you discreetly step out of the line that leads to the female cashier who's sporting a masculine haircut and wearing men's clothes.

Perhaps you're unlike me and you actually go to the gym. Do you refrain from signing up for the Zumba class led by a flamboyant gay man?

On the way to the break room at work, do you take a detour to avoid the cubicle occupied by a lesbian who is outspoken about gay rights?

Even if you are cordial and polite to the LGBT people in your life, could it be because you are merely tolerating them, not because you want to engage in meaningful relationships with them?

Believe me, people from the LGBT community (and a lot of other people) pick up on our slights. It's why the *homophobia* label gets flung at us so much. We're perceived as cold and superior and too scared to even get to know gay people. Worst of all, keeping our distance from people in the LGBT community means we forfeit our chance to influence people for Jesus.

I have a radical suggestion to make. Let's have a *touching impact* on people from the LGBT community. I mean hug and embrace and shake hands, but also touch others with our kindness and compassion, touch them with our friendship, touch them with our presence. There's no quicker way to break down the barriers between us.

I have an advantage in knowing about the importance of touching others with compassion because I once knew a wonderful man named Louis.

My Friend Louis

When my mom and her partner, Vera, would take me to parties for people in the local gay and lesbian community, I usually was the only child present. So for me these events could get boring. My mom knew this, and that's why she would let me go into another room and play video games.

This was the 1980s. We didn't have Nintendo DS or iPads like the pampered youth of today. Instead, back in those days, I had one of the very first Nintendo sets, and I rocked games like *Duck Hunt* and *Kung Fu*. I would lug my big ol' Nintendo game console with me to the house parties that Mom and Vera would take me to.

One evening when I was a grade-schooler, I was sitting on the floor of a bedroom in a house where one of these parties was taking place, and I was playing Nintendo by myself. Then someone poked his head around the corner. It was Louis, a young black man I had met before but hadn't spoken to much. He asked me what I was doing.

"Playing video games," I said without taking my eyes off the screen.

Coming farther into the room, he asked, "What game are you playing?"

"Duck Hunt," I replied. I tell you, those ducks *feared* me.

Louis said, "I get bored with these parties. Do you mind if I play video games with you?"

I was absolutely excited to have somebody shoot ducks with me. And that's how I got to know Louis.

If you had met him, you would have thought he was a heavy-weight boxer. In fact, as I recall him, he reminds me of Evander Holyfield in his prime. Louis was a large guy and he worked out a lot.

He traveled in the same circles that my mother and her partner did, and he was at most of the same parties they were. After that first time, he'd often play video games with me and we'd talk. It turned out we liked the same movies, played the same video games, and fol-lowed the exploits of some of the same superheroes. He was always smiling and kind to me.

Louis was one of the few friends I had when I was growing up, even though he was an adult. I was about to see my friend face some-thing I could barely comprehend.

News No One Wants

One day when I was about eleven, my mom took me to my doctor's office for a routine checkup. And there, sitting in the waiting room, was Louis—he had the same doctor I did. I lit up at the sight of Louis. But I noticed something right away: he looked different. I hadn't seen him in about six months, and now a lot of his muscle was gone and he was thinner. He had a smile on his face, as usual, but it had faded.

I also noticed that Louis had marks on his forehead that looked like bruises. Maybe he even had a couple of open sores on his skin. These marks hadn't been there before, or at least I hadn't noticed them. I tried to ignore them as I walked up to him and gave him a hug.

"Are you feeling okay?" I asked.

Louis looked at me and tears began to well up in his eyes. At that young age, I knew something was wrong, but I had no idea what he was getting ready to unload on me. He kept a smile on his face, wiped some of his tears away, and said, "Caleb, I don't know if you know what this means, but I have AIDS."

This revelation meant nothing to me, but before I could ask what this disease was, a nurse called his name to go in and see our doctor. Louis gave me a thumbs-up as he disappeared behind the door.

I looked over at my mom. She sat there with a stunned look on her face, tears spilling from her eyes. I asked her, "Mom, what's going on?"

"Not now, Caleb. I'll talk to you about it in the car."

At first I thought Louis had something serious but that he would eventually get over it. On our way home from the doctor's office, however, my mother told me what his sickness would do to him. For Louis, this was the beginning of the end.

I began crying and asked my mom why there was nothing any-one could do to save Louis's life.

She said, "There is no cure. However, there's one thing we can give him: our support."

At the Other End of the Room

I didn't see Louis for quite a while. When I did, it was the beginning of the next summer, and I had recently arrived in Kansas City for my usual summertime stay with my mom.

I was sitting in my room at Mom's house, playing video games, when I heard a knock on the door. My mother walked into the room and informed me that Louis had only a few days left to live. That very day, we got in the car and headed over to the hospital to visit him.

What I saw in Louis's hospital room that day I will never forget. It shocked me.

Louis was lying in a bed, and he had obviously lost even more weight than he had the last time I saw him. A shell of the man I had known before, he didn't look anything like Evander Holyfield. He was shivering, and no matter how many blankets the nurses piled on top of him, he could not get warm.

But none of this was the shocking part. What shocked me was his family.

Louis was in a huge room. He lay in a bed at one end of the room, and at the other end were five members of his family. They were about as far away from him as they could possibly be and still share the same room. It was almost as if they were pressed up against the wall, waiting for a firing squad to come. They had their big Bibles out, reading them and discussing what they were reading, but none of them were even paying attention to Louis.

I asked my mom, "Why are they treating him like this? Why aren't they loving him? Why aren't they hugging him?"

My mom replied, "Well, Caleb, they're Christians. You remember what I told you about Christians, right? Christians hate gay people."

Walking over to the bed, I noticed that Louis had no smile on his face. I told him what he meant to me, then threw my arms around him, gave him a kiss on the cheek, and said, "Good-bye, my friend."

The usual smile returned to his face and he said, "I'll see you later, little brother."

As best I can remember, his family never said one word to us. During our time there, they didn't say one word to Louis either. My mom's words rang through my head:

Christians hate gay people.

Christians hate gay people.

Christians hate gay people.

Louis's parents and siblings were afraid to touch him.

Jesus was different.

The Necessary Touch

We've already encountered the religious leaders in stories from the Gospels we've looked at. We already know that the Pharisees and teachers of the Law weren't exactly Jesus's kind of people. So it's good to remind ourselves that in Jesus's day most people in Israel looked up to these religious leaders.

The Pharisees and teachers of the Law knew the Hebrew Scriptures inside and out, and they could cite different interpretations of the Scriptures from various rabbis. Many Pharisees had followers and students. People assumed they were close to God because of how religious they were. They participated in synagogue and temple worship, prayed in public, fasted according to a schedule, taught others how to study the Law, and kept away from people and places that would violate their holiness. Who wouldn't want to be a Pharisee?

Well, Jesus didn't want to be a Pharisee.

As you read through the gospel of Matthew, it doesn't take long before you realize that Jesus didn't admire the Pharisees, nor did he encourage others to emulate them. As a matter of fact, Jesus spent a lot of time preaching against them. Much of the famed Sermon on the Mount (found in Matthew 5–7) is a reaction to the example of the religious leaders of his time. Reread it for yourself with that perspective in mind, and you'll see what I mean.

But right now I want to point out what Jesus did immediately *after* preaching the Sermon on the Mount. After speaking against the example of the Pharisees and teachers of the Law, he demonstrated his differences from them by his actions.

We read in Matthew 8:2 how it started: "A man with leprosy came and knelt before him and said, 'Lord, if you are willing, you can make me clean.'"

Stop right there.

Realize this: no Pharisee would have reached out to this man. He was a leper, and by leaving his leper colony outside the city walls, he was endangering healthy people. What about the germs he might spread? What about those who might be infected by his illness? He was unclean, and the Law clearly stated that he was supposed to be away from the people (see Leviticus 13:45–46). Any good Pharisee would enforce that command.

Jesus, however, was no Pharisee.

What Jesus did next was socially taboo. Actually, if Jesus wanted to be a good rabbi by his culture's standards, what he did next could have been career suicide. "Jesus reached out his hand and touched the man. 'I am willing,' he said. 'Be clean!'" (Matthew 8:3).

Did you see that word? *Touched.*

He *touched* the leper! How in the world could that be? Wasn't

Jesus unclean now? Shouldn't Jesus have gone outside the city gates for a few days?

The thing is, it wasn't just a man who touched this leper. It was God himself. And nothing can make God unclean. God is the one who makes the unclean clean.

But why did Jesus have to touch this man at all? Jesus performed many miracles in different ways, and in some cases Jesus healed without even being around the person. Why in the world did Jesus choose to touch this leper?

I think it was because Jesus knew the man needed it.

While the Old Testament laws that placed the lepers away from the community were for protection, the Pharisees used these laws to treat people poorly. God's Word should never be a catalyst for us to mistreat those who are different from us. For Jesus, touching the leper wasn't about breaking the social taboo in order to be a rebel. It was about ministering to this man's needs. It was about touching and showing affection to someone who hadn't had anyone from outside the leper colony touch him in a long time and who really needed it.

> Nothing can make God unclean. God is the one who makes the unclean clean.

Sometimes we underestimate the power of touch. Don't believe me? Go to a nursing home and give a resident a hug. Go up to your crying child and wrap your arms around her. Put an arm around a person who has experienced emotional trauma and see how he reacts. There's great power in touch. Jesus knew that.

I love the ending of Matthew 8:3: "Immediately he was cleansed of his leprosy." It wasn't a gradual process that resulted in the leper's healing, but rather it was the loving touch of a sovereign God. In that one instant, the man not only was healed physically but also was able to see the love that God had for him.

That's powerful.

That kind of love will change lives.

Thinking back to the hospital room where I last saw Louis, I can only imagine what would have happened if his family had had the same attitude toward him that Jesus had toward the leper. Understand that I'm not calling Louis a leper, but his family certainly treated him as one. In their eyes, he—as a gay man—didn't measure up to what they wanted, and his illness had caused him to be leper-like. The scene in Louis's hospital room would have been much better if they were surrounding him in love and prayer, giving him the comfort of their touch in his last days.

> No matter the person, no matter the circumstance, no matter the issues involved, there are always practical ways to show love to a hurting person.

You might be thinking, *Come on, Caleb. It was the eighties. No one really understood AIDS back then, and you need to cut them a little slack.*

Well, we might not have understood AIDS very well in the 1980s, but we still had the ability to love people. No matter the person, no matter the circumstance, no matter the issues involved, there are always practical ways to show love to a hurting person.

Get Your Hands Dirty

The point of the story of the leper is simple: love those who are outcast or different from you. Don't fear, avoid, or push away those who aren't like you. Love people as God has loved you.

Far from avoiding people from the gay community, as many Christians are tempted to do, you should make a point of getting close to people who are different from you. Spend time with them doing things you both like, as I did in playing video games with Louis. Ask questions to get to know a new friend better. Share your own story. Find some way to be of help. Go to movies, go out to eat, just hang out with people who are different from you. Maybe you could even offer to pray with a person from the LGBT community and begin to dialogue about his or her life. God will use you to demonstrate his love to someone else.

And by the way, this goes both ways. You'll get something back too, as the other person gets to know you in relationship. In fact, I believe we have so much to learn from people from all walks of life, including the LGBT community. Each person carries with him or her vast experiences, joys, hurts, learning, and more. Obviously there will be issues that you will not agree on, but at least you will have a new friend.

In short, you've got to get your hands dirty by embracing the lives of others. Not that people in the LGBT community are actually dirty, any more than the rest of us are. That's just not true. What I'm saying is, if you want to show God's grace to people in this or any community, you've got to get to work at forming relationships with people, one by one. At one point, someone cared enough about you to get his or her hands dirty in the messiness of your life. Maybe it's time for you to do the same for others.

When I became a Christian as a teenager (a story I'll begin to tell in the next chapter), one of the first things I did with my youth group was to go on a summer mission trip. A few of us drove down to Mexico and spent a week building a house for a family that didn't have one.

It was extremely hard work to do in the hot sun. The last phase of building the house was the hardest because that was when we had to put stucco all over the exterior of the house. It was going to take two layers. The day we started the first layer, I must have been running a little late. Everyone else grabbed shovels and other tools to put the stucco on the walls, until all of the tools were gone. *No problem,* I thought. I just put on a pair of gloves and started using my hands to apply the stucco. That's what I did all day.

At night, when we returned to our campsite, I noticed that something was happening to my hands. Some of the stucco had gotten onto my hands and was causing the skin to dry and crack. It was painful. My hands felt raw. I didn't look forward to showing up at the work site the next day for the second round of stucco application, even if I would have a shovel to use.

On the long drive home to Missouri later that week, my hands weren't any better. They still hurt. I thought about what had happened. I mean, surely someone had invented a machine that shoots stucco on a wall without having to get your hands mixed up with the material. Why couldn't I have used a tool like that? I came to the conclusion that in this instance the only way to get the job done had been by getting my hands dirty, and that was okay even if it cost me.

It's time for many of us to get our hands dirty with people who come into our lives, regardless of sexual preference, appearance, economic status, beliefs, or other distinctions.

To this day, I believe that God wanted Louis's family to reach out to him and help him find God. His family had other plans, though. They allowed their fear to keep them away from the mission.

It's our job to treat people better than Louis's family treated him. We have a responsibility to touch them, as if Jesus were reaching out to them with our hands.

REFLECTION AND DISCUSSION QUESTIONS

1. Have you ever known someone who died from AIDS or some kind of horrible disease? Describe your experience.

2. What was so scandalous about Jesus touching this leper of Matthew 8? Why did Jesus touch him? How do you think it felt for the leper to have human contact after so long as an outcast?

3. Who are the "lepers" of today who need to know God's love?

4. Why are so many of us afraid to get our hands messy in the lives of others? What is your greatest fear on this matter? Why is this so?

5. How can you get your hands dirty in the lives of people who are different from you or others who may not know Christ?

No Compromise

U p to this point in the book, we've mostly talked about the necessity for Christians to extend grace to people in the LGBT community. That's the point of *Messy Grace*. But the context won't be complete unless we look at the other side, the truth side.

Yes, we have to be willing to get messy. Yes, we are to pursue others in love, not hate. Yes, we need to lose our us-versus-them mentality. And yes, we are to touch others with the compassion of Jesus. All that's true. And yet it's also true that when it's appropriate to talk about what the Bible says on the topic of homosexuality, we should not hesitate. We should do it with confidence, forthrightness, and a refusal to compromise.

Certainly we should speak the truth in love (see Ephesians 4:15). *But we should speak it.* We don't have to water it down, compromise it, or apologize for it. We don't have the right to change it to make it more palatable according to the prevailing spirit of the age. We have the responsibility to learn and share the truth with graciousness.

To tell you how I came to my conclusions on the truth about God's view of homosexuality, I need to take you back to the time in my life when I first began exploring the subject. Back then, I thought

I was on a secret mission. Little did I know that God was simultaneously on a secret mission pursuing me!

Ninja Christian

It was time. I grabbed a Bible from my dad's bookshelf and held it in my hands. Old and dusty, it had Revised Standard Version printed on the front. I had no idea what that meant. As I opened the book, the spine made a creaking noise.

I was sixteen years old. Up to this point in my life, I had never owned a Bible. I had no idea that there were different translations or that there was even an Old Testament and a New Testament. I just knew that I'd had enough of Christians making fun of my mother and being cruel to people in the LGBT community, like Louis's family had been to him. It was time for me to teach them a lesson.

My plan was simple. I had been formulating it for some time. I would go to a Bible study and attend like I was a Christian. To myself, I called it being a "ninja Christian." I would learn all about Christianity and what Christians believed. I would then take that information and figure out how to dismantle their arguments, because I knew Christianity had to be false.

It just so happened that I had some friends who were trying to share the gospel with me. One of them, named Jeff, invited me to a Bible study at his friend's house. I decided to go, since it seemed like the perfect opportunity to launch my ninja operation.

I was ready to roll.

Standing outside my house, though, I began to get nervous as I waited for Jeff to pick me up. I had never been to a real Bible study before. I had sporadically attended an Episcopal church in Columbia, but we never talked about the Bible at all when I participated in the youth group of that church. So this was all new for me.

Jeff's car approached and I got in. Jeff began to tell me what to expect when I arrived at the Bible study. He said that we might sing a couple of songs and do some prayer before we started talking about the Bible.

Getting even more nervous, I told him I had no idea what any of the songs would be. He just laughed and told me to go with it.

Soon we were parked in front of the house where the Bible study was to be held. After I went inside the house, I was surprised to find that pictures of Jesus were hanging on the walls. There were also pictures of lions and sheep with scripture. What did lions and sheep have to do with the Bible? It was all foreign to me.

When we went downstairs to the basement, where the study was to take place, the group of teens there greeted Jeff. Some of the girls hugged him, and some of the guys asked how his week was. They engaged in small talk. I, meanwhile, remained standing by the stairs, not sure whom I should talk to.

Then the high school student who was the leader of the group came over and introduced himself. He asked me what church I went to, and I told him that I went to an Episcopal church sometimes. I asked him what church he went to (which was weird for me because I'd never asked that question before), and he answered, "The Bible-Believing Fundamentalist Church of Jesus" or something like that.

I smiled and said, "Oh yeah, I know exactly where that is." The truth is, I didn't, but I wanted to act like I fit in. Ninja, remember?

Some other members of the study came up and introduced themselves to me. We all eventually sat down and the leader asked for "prayer requests." I leaned over to Jeff and asked him what this was about. He said that prayer requests were opportunities for us to ask the group to pray for something on our behalf.

Someone asked me, "Caleb, do you have any prayer requests?"

"I'm good at this point," I told him.

Prayer time was bizarre to me. I was used to the *Book of Common Prayer.* It made sense to me because all of the prayers were written out and you just read them and then moved on to the next part of the worship service. The idea of actually talking to God on my own—having a personal conversation with him—was something I had never encountered before.

After prayer time, we turned to the Bible and started studying. The leader referred to some chapter in the Bible, but I was not sure where it was. Everyone was looking at 2 Corinthians, while I was in 2 Chronicles. I figured maybe I'd gotten the wrong Bible. I looked back at the cover, where it said "Revised Standard Version," and I thought, *Wow, they must have updated this over the years.* Nothing the others were saying was matching anything I was reading.

Then someone had the bright idea that we should all go around and read different verses in the chapter.

Now I gulped.

They were all reading these nice verses from the apostle Paul out of 2 Corinthians, and when they got to me, I read an awkward verse from 2 Chronicles. Everyone looked at me like I was a moron. Well, not everyone. Jeff and the leader knew I was brand-new to this.

"Where are you, Caleb?" one of the members of the study asked.

"Uh, I'm not sure. I must have one of those new Bibles or something," I said as I thumbed through pages.

Immediately, I felt like even more of an idiot than before. *"New Bible"? Give me a break, Kaltenbach!* I could feel my ninja disguise slipping.

"Bro, you're probably new to this, so you're gonna want to go to the New Testament and go over a few books to find where we are," the leader encouraged.

"New Testament?" I asked.

"Yes, *the* New Testament," a girl in the group said in a sarcastic tone.

"Wow, um, okay," I said, frustrated at her attitude but trying not to show it. "Well, if there's a New Testament, there must be an Old one too, right?"

I think at this point most of the members got the fact that I was no Christian but rather a "seeker." The girl who had made the sarcastic comment looked down as if she had made a big mistake. Jeff smiled at me, reassuring me that it would be okay. The leader of the study said, "Don't worry about this, Caleb. We've all been new to this at some point or another."

I just smiled and said, "Go ahead and skip me for now. I'll just listen."

Being a ninja Christian, or a seeker, or whatever I was sure made a guy feel awkward.

On the way home, Jeff asked me what I thought about the Bible study.

I lied and told him that I thought it was phenomenal. Inside, though, I was thinking it was anything but phenomenal. It was a bunch of know-it-all Christians who thought I should be exactly where they were in knowledge of the Bible. The way some of them acted toward me was not on the same level as the people who hold up signs on street corners condemning gay people, but it was definitely annoying. Really, what it did more than anything else was convince me that I needed to return and go on the attack against this group and other people who thought they knew who God was.

I did keep going back to this Bible study, and after a while I realized something was happening inside me. I wasn't so sure of things I had once believed. The worldview I had come to attack was not what I thought it was. The Jesus of the Bible was very different from the portrayal of him reflected by some of his followers. He was somebody who was kind and loving and yet still spoke the truth.

Even though I didn't like Christians, when I read Jesus's words in the Bible, they ripped me apart. A big part of me wanted to call a halt because I felt like I was being drawn away from what my parents had brought me up to believe about life. Yet as much as I tried, I couldn't stop learning and thinking about Jesus. I wanted to confront the Christians in this group and ask aggressive questions about their faith, but I just started liking Jesus more than any Christian I had met.

I was still left with a big issue, though. Even though I was beginning to like Jesus, I had to dig in and find out specifically what the Bible said about my mom and other gay people (which included my dad, though I didn't know it at the time). In other words, what did the Bible say about homosexuality? I knew that if I were going to eventually follow Jesus, I would need to understand this issue from a biblical basis.

So, What Does the Bible Say About Homosexuality?

As I began to study what the Bible says about homosexuality, I really struggled with it. Honestly, I still struggle with it because the grace side of me wants to say, "It doesn't matter how we live—just love God." But I know that God doesn't say that. He has standards for sexual relationships as well as all the other areas of our lives. When we live up to these standards, we honor God, and in the end it's good for us too.

But now, before we go further, I want to reiterate that I'm no scholar. I don't have a PhD, nor have I written books on New Testament backgrounds or studies. I just want to give you a synopsis of what I've come to believe the Bible says about homosexuality. If you want to study this topic in more depth, I suggest you check out the works listed under "More Reading" at the end of this book.

Also, I want to say that I understand this is a point in the book where you may be tempted to switch from thinking *I agree with all of this* to concluding *Now Caleb's gone to the conservative side.* But what I say here is fully consistent with everything I've already said.

Typically, when we wrestle with the tension of grace and truth, we either go all the way to the grace side, where everything is deemed acceptable, or we go all the way to the truth side, where we speak truth and have no love. It's harder to live in the tension of grace and truth. Yet that is just what this chapter is doing, just like the rest of the book.

With all that in mind, here is what a teenage ninja began to discover about what the Bible says about homosexuality.

The Male-Female Relationship

At the beginning of the Bible, we read that God created Adam first and then Eve. Then we see how God orchestrated the first marriage between these two:

> For Adam no suitable helper was found. So the LORD God
> caused the man to fall into a deep sleep; and while he was
> sleeping, he took one of the man's ribs and then closed up the
> place with flesh. Then the LORD God made a woman from

the rib he had taken out of the man, and he brought her to
the man.

The man said,

"This is now bone of my bones
    and flesh of my flesh;
she shall be called 'woman,'
    for she was taken out of man."

That is why a man leaves his father and mother and
is united to his wife, and they become one flesh. (Genesis
2:20–24)

This sets the precedent for what God has established as an acceptable sexual relationship.

Now, there are those who see this story as theological fiction, not
real history, and so they may resist drawing too strong a conclusion
from it. Yet isn't it interesting that Jesus himself quoted this passage
and seemed to take it seriously as history (see Matthew 19:4–5;
Mark 10:6–8)? The apostle Paul seemed to take this as a real event
as well, referring to Adam as a historical person (see Romans
5:12–21).

Even if the Adam and Eve story wasn't historical fact and we
were justified in dismissing it, we would have to realize that a precedent was set through this "metaphorical story": biblical sexuality is
expressed between male and female. The same normative pattern of
intimacy between a man and a woman is taught elsewhere in the
Scriptures. For example, Paul said in Ephesians 5:22–33:

Wives, submit yourselves to your own husbands as you do to
the Lord. For the husband is the head of the wife as Christ is

the head of the church, his body, of which he is the Savior. Now as the church submits to Christ, so also wives should submit to their husbands in everything.

Husbands, love your wives, just as Christ loved the church and gave himself up for her to make her holy, cleansing her by the washing with water through the word, and to present her to himself as a radiant church, without stain or wrinkle or any other blemish, but holy and blameless. In this same way, husbands ought to love their wives as their own bodies. He who loves his wife loves himself. After all, no one ever hated their own body, but they feed and care for their body, just as Christ does the church—for we are members of his body. "For this reason a man will leave his father and mother and be united to his wife, and the two will become one flesh." This is a profound mystery—but I am talking about Christ and the church. However, each one of you also must love his wife as he loves himself, and the wife must respect her husband.

Do you see how Paul assumed that an intimate relationship is between a man and a woman? Furthermore, Paul clearly communicated a doctrine that intimacy between men and women is a picture of the intimacy Jesus has with his church.

Paul did something similar in 1 Corinthians 7:1–5:

Now for the matters you wrote about: "It is good for a man not to have sexual relations with a woman." But since sexual immorality is occurring, each man should have sexual relations with his own wife, and each woman with her own husband. The husband should fulfill his marital duty to his

wife, and likewise the wife to her husband. The wife does
not have authority over her own body but yields it to her
husband. In the same way, the husband does not have
authority over his own body but yields it to his wife. Do not
deprive each other except perhaps by mutual consent and for
a time, so that you may devote yourselves to prayer. Then
come together again so that Satan will not tempt you
because of your lack of self-control.

Here, Paul described the male-female relationship and gave advice in marriage. He briefly discussed the role that spirituality plays
in the marriage relationship and how God designed the husband and
wife to be in an intimate relationship together.

When we study the Bible in depth on this matter, we see that it
is unified in its teaching that appropriate intimacy is between men
and women.

Homosexuality and Sin

If intimacy is supposed to be between men and women, then what
does the Bible say about homosexuality? Several stories and teaching
passages in the Scriptures categorically identify sexual relations between persons of the same gender as sin (which means "missing the
mark").

First, let's deal with the ancient story that gives us our word
sodomy.

We need to be careful with this one. Many Christians have misinterpreted Genesis 19 to mean that Sodom and Gomorrah were
destroyed because of the sin of homosexuality. Actually, however,
God destroyed these cities for a range of sins, as he explained through
the prophet Ezekiel: "Now this was the sin of your sister Sodom: She

and her daughters were arrogant, overfed and unconcerned; they did not help the poor and needy. They were haughty and did detestable things before me. Therefore I did away with them as you have seen" (16:49–50). Homosexuality isn't specifically mentioned here.

Nevertheless, the account of this event back in Genesis does say that the men of Sodom were aggressively seeking to have sex with Lot's visitors (angels who had taken the appearance of human males). Lot called the men's request a "wicked thing" (19:7), another way of saying it was sinful. (Unfortunately, Lot offered an equally wicked thing by suggesting that the men of Sodom take his two virgin daughters. Let that be a lesson to those of us who think culture can't negatively influence the thinking of those trying to live for God.)[5]

Later on in the Old Testament, God says specifically that homosexuality is forbidden. In the context of a whole range of sexual sins, sexual relations between men (and by implication, between women too) is prohibited:

Do not have sexual relations with a man as one does with a woman; that is detestable. (Leviticus 18:22)

If a man has sexual relations with a man as one does with a woman, both of them have done what is detestable. (20:13)

Other verses in the Old Testament criticize cross-dressing (see Deuteronomy 22:5) and the homosexual prostitution that was sometimes a part of pagan religion (see 1 Kings 15:12; 22:46; 2 Kings 23:7).

Now, some people will say the Old Testament prohibition against sex with someone of the same gender is not valid today because we are no longer under the Law. They sometimes use arguments like "So it's okay for you to eat shellfish, but we can't define our sexuality however we want? How can you pick and choose what to obey and what not to obey?"

My answer is, it's not the same thing. When you look in the New Testament, you find that Jesus declared that all foods are clean (see Mark 7:19). Nowhere in the New Testament, however, does God define acceptable sexuality as being other than between one man and one woman. In fact, the New Testament specifically reaffirms the Old Testament's position that same-gender sexual activity is not acceptable.

The most prominent example is in Romans 1:26–27. These verses come in a context where the apostle Paul was giving a historical and theological explanation for human sin and separation from God. Having sex with someone of the same gender is far from being the only sin he cited as an example, but it's a prominent one:

> God gave them over to shameful lusts. Even their women
> exchanged natural sexual relations for unnatural ones. In the
> same way the men also abandoned natural relations with
> women and were inflamed with lust for one another. Men
> committed shameful acts with other men, and received in
> themselves the due penalty for their error.

Some people in recent years have tried to make the argument that traditional interpreters of this passage have misunderstood the word *natural* here. They say that whatever intimate relationship you have is natural as long as it is natural to you. So, in this line of thinking, if a same-sex relationship seems natural to you, then what Paul said in Romans 1:26–27 cannot be applied to your life. It applies only if you are in a relationship that seems unnatural to you.

This view, however, doesn't hold up.

The scholar John Stott explained the Romans 1 passage and said the word "*physis* ('natural') means God's created order. To act 'against nature' means to violate the order which God has established, whereas to act 'according to nature' means to behave 'in accordance with the intention of the Creator.' Moreover, the intention of the Creator means His original intention."[6] In other words, Paul was saying that God is the only one who gets to define what is natural and what isn't. One can clearly see the natural order in Genesis 2:24, where marriage is identified as being between a man and a woman.

Alternatively, some try to reframe Paul's words here by appealing to the historical context in which Paul was writing. They say that he was referring to homosexual temple prostitution or that he was speaking of abusive relationships rather than monogamous same-sex relationships.

Yet Paul never specifically limited his focus. Rather, he seemed to be speaking about same-sex relationships as a whole. If Paul were talking only about a specific type of homosexual relationships, why did he paint a broad sweep of sin in Romans 1:28–32?

> Just as they did not think it worthwhile to retain the knowledge of God, so God gave them over to a depraved mind, so that they do what ought not to be done. They have become filled with every kind of wickedness, evil, greed and depravity. They are full of envy, murder, strife, deceit and malice. They are gossips, slanderers, God-haters, insolent, arrogant and boastful; they invent ways of doing evil; they disobey their parents; they have no understanding, no fidelity, no love, no

mercy. Although they know God's righteous decree that those who do such things deserve death, they not only continue to do these very things but also approve of those who practice them.

Those who interpret Romans 1:21–27 as referring only to temple prostitution or something of that nature (and say that it has nothing to do with monogamous LGBT relationships) have to do fancy footwork with the historical context. And if an argument rests mostly on historical context, with little literary context to back it up, we need to be careful about trusting that kind of evidence.[7]

Confirming Paul's view on homosexuality, two other passages in his writings situate sexually active gay men and lesbians within lists of other types of sinners.

> Do you not know that wrongdoers will not inherit the kingdom of God? Do not be deceived: Neither the sexually immoral nor idolaters nor adulterers *nor men who have sex with men* nor thieves nor the greedy nor drunkards nor slanderers nor swindlers will inherit the kingdom of God. And that is what some of you were. But you were washed, you were sanctified, you were justified in the name of the Lord Jesus Christ and by the Spirit of our God. (1 Corinthians 6:9–11)

> We know that the law is good if one uses it properly. We also know that the law is made not for the righteous but for lawbreakers and rebels, the ungodly and sinful, the unholy and irreligious, for those who kill their fathers or mothers, for murderers, for the sexually immoral, *for those practicing homosexuality,* for slave traders and liars and perjurers—and for whatever else is contrary to the sound doctrine that

conforms to the gospel concerning the glory of the blessed
God, which he entrusted to me. (1 Timothy 1:8–11)

The conclusion from all this seems obvious to me. The apostle
Paul consistently condemned having sex with someone of the same
gender, reinforcing what the Hebrew Scriptures already said.

Jesus and Homosexuality

Some people, after stating that the Old Testament Law is passé and
the apostle Paul is misinterpreted, think their strongest point is that
Jesus never condemned homosexuality. Their assumption is that
whatever the rest of the Bible may or may not say about homosexuality, as long as Jesus was okay with homosexuality, then so should we
be. I've heard this line of reasoning often.

A couple of years after I became a Christian, I went to a GLAAD
event with my mom. One of the women attending the event was the
academic dean at a theologically liberal seminary, and without my
knowing it, my mom asked her to challenge my new views on sexuality. So the woman came over to me and started talking about the
Bible and homosexuality.

This scholar asked what I thought, and I told her that at one
point in my life I didn't think there was anything wrong with homosexuality, but that after reading the Bible my view had changed.

I'll never forget what she said: "The Bible doesn't say anything
negative about it."

I quoted book, chapter, and verse from the Word on homosexuality, including many of the same verses I've listed here.

Her response? "Those instances aside, Jesus never said anything."

I couldn't let that go. I brought up the fact that Jesus defined
the boundaries of sexuality as being between a husband and wife,

consistent with the rest of Scripture. Jesus said, "At the beginning the Creator 'made them male and female,' and said, 'For this reason a man will leave his father and mother and be united to his wife, and the two will become one flesh'" (Matthew 19:4–5). Another way to say this is that Jesus had the chance to define an intimate relationship as being other than male-female, but he did not.

I also reminded the dean that Jesus did use an umbrella term for sexual immorality.[8] So in that sense, it's fair to argue that he referred to homosexuality.

From there, I went on to mention the danger in relying on what logicians call an argument from silence. I said, "Jesus never said anything about drugs and gangs. So, does that make those things okay?"

Last, I pointed out that one of the reasons Jesus may not have addressed homosexual behavior as loudly as Paul did could have been because Jesus was sent to Israel. The first-century Jewish community, following Old Testament Law, consistently disapproved of homosexuality, so it wasn't much of an issue for them. But when Paul was sent to the Gentiles, all of a sudden the subject became important to Christian teaching, since homosexuality was much more accepted in Roman culture.

I don't believe I moved the academic dean at all, but neither did she move me. I still think I was right. It's completely unwarranted to portray Jesus as being in favor of homosexuality.

More than that, I have a problem with the way some people try to oppose the Gospels to the rest of Scripture, apparently assuming that if they can make Jesus out to be for or against something they are for or against, then it doesn't matter what the rest of the Bible says about it. That's the wrong way to go about using the Bible.

Now, I can accept that some passages in the Bible have little application to our lives today. Don't believe me? Check out some of the food listings in Leviticus and get back to me on that. However, when someone says we need to listen to what Jesus says more than what Paul says, I have to disagree. All Scripture is equally inspired, no matter who wrote or said it (see 2 Timothy 3:16).

A Universal Truth

Some people dismiss everything the Bible says about homosexuality, writing it all off as cultural interpretation that doesn't apply today. But it's far safer to let Scripture itself give us clues as to when some practice or prohibition was culturally limited. For instance, in 1 Corinthians 11, Paul instructed women to keep their heads covered when practicing their faith around others, especially men. The words are clear enough on their face, yet Paul didn't repeat that instruction anywhere else in his writings. Peter, James, and John didn't deal with it either. This suggests to us that what Paul said about coverings was cultural and limited to a particular time and place. On the other hand, Paul and other writers of the Bible on a number of occasions spoke of how sexual intimacy is between a man and a woman.

The fact that all the Bible writers are in agreement on this issue doesn't make it cultural. Rather, it makes it universal.

God defines sexual intimacy between one man and one woman.

Now, I know that you may totally disagree with my conclusion on this matter. You may feel in your heart that if somebody wants to actively identify as LGBT, then what business is it of ours? I get it. I was once there myself. And I would be the first to say that everyone is entitled to his or her own opinion. Also, a person's personal and sexual life is (to some degree) between that person and God.

The thing is, ultimately it doesn't matter what you and I think. It matters what God thinks.

It's tremendously hard for me to write that people I love have been living in a way that is wrong. After growing up in the LGBT community, believing there's nothing wrong with homosexuality, and dearly loving people who are still in the gay community, I tremble as I write these words. First, because I don't want to turn them off. Second, because I fear there are many who know what the Bible says and just don't care. But I have committed myself to God through Christ, and I have to affirm what God affirms.

> Ultimately it doesn't matter what you and I think. It matters what God thinks.

When people study the Bible, they often bring their own presuppositions and biases with them and they see all verses through a certain lens. There are a lot of emotions, history, pain, and more that come attached with the discussion of homosexuality. What I want to ask you to do is to put aside your biases and feelings and just study what the Bible says in its literary and historical contexts. That, I believe, is the way to approach the issue.

If you're sharp enough, you can interpret the Bible to allow most anything you want. That's what I'm *not* trying to do. I'm not going off of my own personal opinion. If there was anyone who wanted the Bible to agree with my parents' view of sexuality, it was me! If there was anyone who wanted to massage Greek words, manipulate exegesis, or read into historical context to force the Bible to say what I wanted it to, it was most definitely me!

With this issue, I'm trying my best to stand on the authority of God's Word. If you don't agree with what I'm saying, that's fine, but use the Bible and tell me where I am wrong. Study passages and come up with a firm decision. Look at what the Bible has to say systematically about this issue. I appreciate that people have their opinions, but for those of us who live as disciples of Jesus, feelings alone don't get you very far. We need to base our opinions on Scripture.

When Beliefs Change

Many of us believe in Jesus and in the reliability of the Bible. We were taught from a young age what the Bible says about how to live our lives. We know what's right and wrong. We know what God values. But when it comes to upholding those values, we falter.

It's not hard to hold to biblical beliefs when we are in the comfort of Sunday school rooms with flannel graphs. But then we get into the world and things are different. We go to schools and jobs and we're confronted with people who have differing worldviews on many issues.

It's so easy to lie about our beliefs, not be truthful, or maybe even change our beliefs. It's incredibly easy to change when it seems the entire world is saying that homosexuality is good, natural, loving, and okay. It's easy to go with the changing tide, and it's difficult to go against popular belief and be labeled as hateful or bigoted.

A lot of people I know have had friends and family members who have come out to them, and they don't know what to do. They know what the Bible has to say about actively being in a same-sex relationship, but they don't know how to reconcile that with their friendships. As a matter of fact, I can bet that most Christians I know who have changed their view on this tender issue have done so because someone they love came out to them.

Senator Rob Portman of Ohio became a prominent example of this transition. Portman supported the view that marriage is only between a man and a woman . . . until his son came out to him. Then his views changed.

"I have come to believe that if two people are prepared to make a lifetime commitment to love and care for each other in good times and in bad, the government shouldn't deny them the opportunity to get married," Portman wrote in a statement.

He then wrote, "That isn't how I've always felt. As a Congressman, and more recently as a Senator, I opposed marriage for same-sex couples. Then, something happened that led me to think through my position in a much deeper way." [9]

Notice his wording: "That isn't how I've always felt" and "Something happened." Senator Portman felt one way, then someone he loved came out to him and he chose to reconcile the difference by changing his belief system.

> Why do people change their view on same-sex relationships? In most cases, it's because someone they love has come out to them and it no longer fits their worldview.

We are used to politicians changing their minds, right? Recently, however, many others have joined the ranks of those who used to think one way about same-sex relationships and now think a completely different way. Some recent scholars who were seen as part of the conservative theologian crowd have changed their minds because their children or other people they know have come out of the closet. Some of these professors have written entire books on why they've taken a different position, and they do some fancy exegetical and theological footwork to back up their claims that the Bible doesn't say anything negative about monogamous same-sex relationships.

Pastors, likewise, have announced to their churches that they no longer view marriage as limited to the heterosexual option.

Why do people change their view on same-sex relationships? In most cases, it's because someone they love has come out to them and it no longer fits their worldview.

When people we love come to us and tell us about a part of their life that is out of line with Scripture, we have some choices: We can kick them out of our life. We can ignore it. We can change our beliefs so there's no tension between us. Or we can keep loving them and hold our beliefs firm.

> There's no reason believers should change orthodox beliefs on what Scripture says in order to keep a relationship with another person.

For me, the last option has always worked the best.

We live in a time when we will be called bigots and narrow-minded for holding on to what we believe the Bible says. I say, "So be it." Remember that when we live in the tension of grace and truth, there will be times when we side with grace and seem overly gracious. Then when we side with the truth of an issue, those same people who thought we were too gracious may now think we're too strict. If that seems confusing and maybe even a bit uncomfortable, that means you're starting to understand how the tension is necessary to walk in and harder than simply always siding with grace or truth.

I believe the tension proves that you can't have real grace without truth, and you can't have real truth without grace. In this instance, we're leaning heavily on the truth side.

We can and must hold true to what we believe God's Word says on any issue, including this one. It is possible to love others and not agree with areas in which they live their life. It is possible to be like Jesus, stay committed to God's way, and still be a light in their life. There's no reason believers should change orthodox beliefs on what Scripture says in order to keep a relationship with another person.

We can stand for truth.

We can unite in grace.

We can love the person.

We can stay in a relationship with them.

We can live in the tension of grace and truth.

We can and we should.

REFLECTION AND DISCUSSION QUESTIONS

1. Do you agree that God desires sexuality to be expressed only between a man and a woman? Why or why not?

2. Look at some of the passages mentioned in this chapter. Why are they so hard for some of us to accept? Are there any that you struggle with accepting? Why or why not?

3. In the past, have you changed your belief on what God thinks about sexuality? Why or why not?

4. Why do you think some people change their minds on what they think of sexuality? Does culture play a role in this decision?

5. When we wrestle with the tension of grace and truth, how can we best handle the truth side?

The Marriage
of Grace and Truth

s it possible to hold on to one's beliefs in regard to a biblical view of sexuality and still love a person who is actively in a same-sex relationship?

As we saw in the last chapter, *yes!*

Look at the people Jesus loved even while they were still living a life contrary to what God said (these are just a few examples):

- Zacchaeus
- Matthew
- Roman centurions
- The adulterous woman from John 8
- Nicodemus
- The disciples

Jesus was able to love these people and yet still hold on to his beliefs. Nowhere in the Bible do I notice Jesus trying to align his beliefs with what the world believed. That's what made him stand out from culture. Dare I say that's what made him so interesting to people?

Nor did he give up on people who were far from God. He continued to love them and pursue them. Even when he had good reasons to walk away and align himself with religious leaders, he chose to continue down the path of grace and truth.

As we continue our journey, I want to make the point that knowing and embracing biblical truth about same-sex issues should make us *more loving toward the LGBT community than ever*. Far from the image that many in the LGBT community have of conservative Christians hating them, we should be gracious to the community all the more because we know that not only are they sinners (like us) but also God loves them. We should be *more* loving toward the gay community than we were before we became followers of Jesus. We should be *more* loving toward people who are not followers of Jesus at all.

This is where it becomes hard, because it's always tough to hold two strong claims (in this case, grace and truth) with equal determination. Here's where it becomes messy, too, because in the real world, how do we know the right way to show love without compromising truth?

> Knowing and embracing biblical truth about same-sex issues should make us *more loving toward the LGBT community than ever.*

Although I hadn't fully articulated all this to myself when I first started considering Jesus's claims, these were truly the issues uppermost in my mind.

Ready

After the Bible study I described in the last chapter, I started going to a local church so I could learn more about how to attack Christianity. I found out there was a huge difference between this church and the church I grew up in. In his sermons, the pastor, Max, explained Bible passages verse by verse. I had never seen this before. Max also had an authority when he preached that I had not noticed in other pastors. To this day, I credit Max with piquing my interest in becoming a pastor.

I started attending the youth group of this church. The fellowship of this group was incredible, and I gained so many friends. Furthermore, when I learned there was a really sharp campus minister at the University of Missouri–Columbia, I started going to his Bible study to learn more about Scripture. This man literally had the Bible memorized. I attended his study as much as I could because I had never known anyone as intelligent as this person.

I felt like I was getting so much knowledge on the Bible. I was attending church, participating in a youth group, and even going to a Bible study at the university. I had gotten more than I bargained for when I first set out to attack Christianity. When my parents would attack Christians and the Christian faith, I started keeping my mouth shut.

Quickly, the people in my youth group became like family to me. We went on trips together, hung out together, and exchanged gifts at Christmas. When I wasn't spending time with people in the group, I was studying the Bible.

The funniest thing happened in the middle of all this: I started to really like Jesus. As a matter of fact, I even wanted to know what it was like to follow him. I decided to call a Christian friend named Gregg (a fellow high school student and the son of Pastor Max). I said to him on the phone, "I'm ready to see what it means to follow Jesus."

The First Day of the Rest of My Life

Gregg and I agreed to meet at a Chinese restaurant. I got there ahead of him and ordered a meal. While I waited for it to come, I sat at a table wondering what I would say. I knew that if I made a decision to really give Jesus my all, it would put barriers between me and my parents and our relationship might never be the same. Even though my dad had not yet come out to me, I knew that he had negative opinions of conservative Christians. He wouldn't respond well to my decision to follow Jesus. At that time in my life, those thoughts were a lot to handle. I was actually thinking about walking out of the restaurant when the front door opened and Gregg was there.

He strolled in with a big black binder and sat down at the table. Gregg had brown hair and a muscular physique, as you would expect of a star on the football and basketball teams at our school. I wasn't used to the "cool kids" showing much attention to me, but Gregg was a good friend, and now he was prepared to have the most important conversation of my life with me.

Gregg didn't order anything other than a drink. He got right down to business, opening up the binder and beginning to explain the plan of salvation to me. Using verses from Romans, he showed me that I had sinned and was living apart from God but that Jesus had provided a chance for me to live with God forever.

My food arrived in the midst of this presentation, but I couldn't eat. I used my fork to push around the sweet-and-sour chicken on my plate as if my stomach might get hungrier if I saw my food move. But I just stared at the chicken while listening to what Gregg had to say.

Then, as Gregg was talking, it happened. I can't explain it. Something just shifted inside me. I truly believed what he was saying. There was no way around it—in that moment I became a follower of Jesus.

Gregg was in midsentence when I cut him off and said, "Look, I already believe this. What's my next step?"

With a big smile on his face, he told me that people who believe in Jesus get baptized.

Not knowing much about Scripture or theology, I suggested we go to the church immediately so I could get baptized. "Would you baptize me, Gregg? I don't think my parents would approve, and I just want to do this—I know that God wants me to do this."

Gregg agreed and we were on our way.

There were only three witnesses to my baptism: Gregg, the church administrator, and a church secretary. Walking into the baptistery, Gregg told me there was nothing about the water that would save me. Rather, it was God's grace acting in my commitment to Christ that had already saved me. I was just showing the world who my Lord and Savior was.

I still recall what it felt like to be baptized. Even though it lasted only seconds, in my mind it was slow motion. When I was placed under the water, I imagined being buried as Christ was buried. When I was brought up out of the water, I imagined that the water rolling off my face symbolized my purity before God. I heard the applause of only two people in the auditorium, but Gregg assured me there was a party in heaven going on right at that moment.

As I dried off in the back room, Gregg told me all about how I could get more involved in the church. I'd like to say I was listening to him, but all that was going through my mind were thoughts about my parents. I knew they would not be happy about what had happened. I also knew what the Bible had to say about homosexuality, and I knew what my parents believed about homosexuality. My mom was loud and proud about her sexuality, and my dad was very outspoken against conservative Christians and supporting the LGBT community. In my mind, I had no idea how to reconcile the two. My head was filled with questions about what I was going to do with my parents.

Gregg and I walked out of the church and back to his car. My hair was still wet from the baptism. In my hand I clutched my first Bible. I hadn't owned a Bible before, but Gregg had grabbed one from the church's stash and had written in it, commemorating this occasion for me. I felt like a new person.

But I knew the decision I had made would cost me.

We got in his car and Gregg started driving me back home, where I would have to tell my dad what I had done. I looked at Gregg as he was driving and asked him, "How?"

He looked at me and said, "How what?"

"How in the world," I asked, "do you reconcile my mom's relationship with Vera and the Bible?"

There was a long pause.

Gregg replied, "You can't stop loving her, Caleb. She and Vera are your family, and you cannot stop your love for them. If anything, becoming a follower of Jesus should make you love them all the more."

I knew he was right.

We drove up to my house and he let me out. Rolling down the window, he yelled, "Praying for you!" as he drove off down the street.

Then it was just me.

I stood there clutching my Bible as I stared at the house. I had gone in there under many different circumstances in the past. This time, it would be the hardest circumstance I'd ever faced. In my head, I tried to imagine God surrounding me with his presence as I was about to go in the house.

The long walk up to the front door had started.

My mission was just beginning.

Love That Never Stops

When I started going to the new church, one of the first sermons I heard was on the parable of the prodigal son (see Luke 15:11–32). Here, Jesus was preaching to a mixed crowd. His listeners included Pharisees, other religious leaders, "sinners," and people who were on the fringes of society.

Jesus told a story about a father who is wealthy and has two sons. His oldest son is prideful and does everything his father wants. The younger son is independent and always thinking of himself.

When the younger son is old enough, he asks his father for his inheritance. Back in that day, it would be like telling your father to drop dead because you just want his money.

If that didn't shock Jesus's original listeners, then the next part of the story would. The father actually does what the younger son wants! More than likely he gives the firstborn two-thirds of the inheritance and the younger son one-third.

The younger son leaves and goes to a distant country. In other words, he goes to party. He takes his inheritance (which is a lot of money) and blows it in a place like Vegas. He has a lot of fun, a lot of girlfriends, and a lot of other friends.

When the money runs out, all of a sudden his friends are nowhere to be found. Also, he can't find any work because he is in a foreign country. So he does the lowest thing imaginable: he sells himself out to a pig farmer. Working with pigs was not a good thing in the minds of Jewish people back in Jesus's day. They considered these animals to be unclean.

The younger son hits rock bottom when he ends up wanting to eat the same food that the pigs are eating. In this moment he knows he needs a change in his life.

He comes up with an incredible idea, saying to himself, "How many of my father's hired servants have food to spare, and here I am starving to death! I will set out and go back to my father and say to him: Father, I have sinned against heaven and against you. I am no longer worthy to be called your son; make me like one of your hired servants" (Luke 15:17–19). At least he would eat better and he would be in a familiar place.

He starts the journey home, probably practicing his speech over and over again. After a long walk, he sees his dad's house in the distance. Something then happens that he wasn't expecting:

> While he was still a long way off, his father saw him and was filled with compassion for him; he ran to his son, threw his arms around him and kissed him.
>
> The son said to him, "Father, I have sinned against heaven and against you. I am no longer worthy to be called your son."
>
> But the father said to his servants, "Quick! Bring the best robe and put it on him. Put a ring on his finger and sandals on his feet. Bring the fattened calf and kill it. Let's have a feast and celebrate. For this son of mine was dead and is alive again; he was lost and is found." So they began to celebrate. (verses 20–24)

There's more to the story, but I want to stop right here and focus on the father's reaction. I want to point out that the father never stopped loving the son.

Read that again . . .

The father never stopped loving the son.

Even when the son basically told the father to drop dead, the father still loved him. Even when the son took the money and left, the father still loved him. Even when the son spent all the money recklessly, the father still loved him. Even when the son sold himself to a pig farmer, the father still loved him. The love of the father had no end.

The father in this story of course represents God. So for those of us who are in Christ, we can be sure that God doesn't stop loving us. We can't outrun or outdo the love of God. *His love doesn't depend on our behavior.* If God's love depended on how I act, I would have been out of God's favor a while ago—and you would have too.

We can't behave or work our way into God's grace. God's love depends on his Son, who died on the cross for our sins. God is satisfied with Jesus's sacrifice, so when we believe in his Son, God delights in us. God loves us because of his Son.

> We can't outrun or outdo the love of God. *His love doesn't depend on our behavior.*

But guess what? Even *before* a person is a Christian, God is still full of love for him or her. Here is a familiar verse that proves this point: "God so loved the world that he gave his one and only Son, that whoever believes in him shall not perish but have eternal life" (John 3:16). We've got to pay attention to the wording here. God doesn't just love people who have chosen to follow him. He loves "the world." He loves people who don't know him, perhaps hate him, and live very differently from the way he wishes they would.

Christians need to have this same kind of love—a love that is not only for other Christians who are different or who may be struggling but is also for those who aren't Christians at all! This is the kind of love that is patient and allows people to be themselves as they begin to discover who they are (or can be) in Jesus Christ. This love is founded in the messy marriage of grace and truth.

Acceptance Without Approval

I wasn't going to have an easy time showing love to my parents. (You'll see what I mean in the next chapter.) I dare say you won't have an easy time showing love to unbelievers in your life either, regardless of their story. Over time, however, I have discovered a distinction that will help us hold on to both grace and truth in our relationships with people who do not know Christ: We can *accept* others as friends or family without *approving* of their life choices.

I know for a fact that every Sunday I shake hands with men who have secretly been on websites they shouldn't be on, and yet I still accept them. I know there are women who greet me on Sunday morning just after gossiping about someone else. I can accept the person who has huge jealousy issues and not agree with his choices. I'm still friends with people who have anger issues, and yet I don't agree with what they do. You and I can have a relationship with somebody who is hooked on drugs and still not approve of the choices this person makes. I have lots of friends who struggle with pride, and yet I haven't given up on them.

What I'm talking about is *accepting,* which is different from *ap-*

proving. To approve of something means that you're throwing your support behind an action, a lifestyle, or a thing. It's possible to accept people without approving of their decisions or how they live life. Jesus did it all the time. If you look at the Gospels and the unbelievers Jesus interacted with, he was always showing love to them and spending time with them, but he never approved of any kind of sin that people would commit. Yet that never stopped him from loving an individual.

Let's switch gears from Jesus's day to our day. When it comes to the LGBT people in our lives . . .

- We can be accepting but not approving.
- We can be loving without applauding.
- We can be compassionate without commending.

In my relationship with my parents after I became a Christian, they eventually realized that I would never change how I felt about them. I always invited them to my house, parties, functions, and so on. Many times, as I got older, they would come to visit me and my family. We still talk weekly on the phone. My parents understood early on that I didn't approve of

> We can *accept* others as friends or family without *approving* of their life choices.

their sexual life choices, but that didn't change our core relationship. It was always the same because my love for them wasn't based on their life choices, and their love for me wasn't based on what I believed about their lifestyle.

You no doubt have people in your life who are doing things or living certain ways that you don't approve of. Chances are, some of these people are friends and family. If you want to follow the example of Jesus, you will not give up on them or love them less. There may come a time for tough love, but you can accept others without approving of what they do or how they live.

Let me give you an example of what I'm talking about.

Five Don'ts and a Do
When Someone Comes Out to You

One of the biggest struggles that some Christians have is how to react when someone they love comes out to them as a gay man or lesbian. They don't know how to react. What are they supposed to feel and not feel? What are they supposed to say and not say?

It's this very moment that has cost people dearly. It's this very moment that has caused divisions in families and friendships. Why? Because some people don't know how to react, and sometimes the person who has come out interprets the immediate reaction as indicative of how these people really feel. I don't think that's always fair. Most people need time to process really big news. But still the reaction to the big reveal is crucial.

That's why I want to help you be prepared, because if you've never had someone come out to you, eventually you will.

First, understand this: it takes a lot of courage for friends or family members to share this part of their life with you. They're risking rejection and misunderstanding. They're risking the relationship itself. As shocked as you may feel, they are equally fearful.

Take that seriously. And furthermore, realize that the mere fact that they came out to you shows how much they love and respect you. They wouldn't necessarily come out to everybody in their life. But because of who you are to them and because of what they think about you, they have chosen you to receive a precious truth about their identity.

So be careful of the first words that come out of your mouth. The best first thing you can say to others when they come out to you is "Thank you."

"Thank you for sharing this part of your life with me."

"Thank you for thinking enough of me to include me in this."

"Thank you for telling me more about you."

"Thank you for trusting me with this part of your life."

This is just the beginning of a conversation, of course, not the whole thing. But if more coming-out conversations started on this note, they would flow better. Unfortunately, most people don't begin with the gracious response of "Thank you." They react very differently, and the conversation winds up being painful on both sides.

Here are some things *not* to do.

Don't Look Disappointed

I can't tell you the number of times I've talked to people who have come out to others and learned that the person they were coming out to had a hurtful look on his or her face. Granted, sometimes this look is more about processing the news, but still it conveys disappointment. That can devastate the person trying to let you into his or her life.

Don't Get Mad

Why would you use this moment to get mad? Unfortunately, many people do. Especially parents. Getting upset about news like this won't help anyone and it will wound your relationship.

Even though you may have a range of emotions, I want to point out that the person coming out to you valued you enough to include you in this part of his or her life. The coming-out conversation is a very personal conversation and can be extremely tough. If you get mad, you will take this moment and throw it away. Unfortunately, you can never get this moment back.

Don't Throw Out Bible Verses

For most Christians, this will be the first reaction they have. "Well, honey, the Bible says . . ." Chances are, the person coming out to you already has a pretty good idea of what the Bible says about the topic. Even people who aren't Christians know that the Bible isn't interpreted by a lot of Christians to be favorable to having a sexual relationship with someone of the same gender. This is not a moment that you need to use to enlighten them. This is a moment to listen.

Don't Compare

I've heard so many Christians say to someone who comes out to them, "I understand that you're gay, and I don't think that is any worse than the sin of murder, theft, adultery, and so on." Wow! Let me say that theologically I believe this is correct. In God's eyes, sin is sin. While sin may carry different earthly consequences, all sin carries the same eternal consequence in that it leads us to eternal separation from God (see Romans 6:23). So this is a correct theological statement.

But we need to be careful about this. I'm not sure this theological idea should be framed in comparison. Why? Because nobody wins in comparison. There may be biblical truth here, but the person on the receiving end thinks, *Okay, so you just compared me to Hannibal Lecter, Gordon Gekko, and other shady characters.* We can be right about theology but wrong in how or when we communicate such truth. You and I can lose the person at the expense of being *right*. I trust that God will give you margin to discuss issues like holy living later in your relationship. That time is not when someone comes out to you. If that person is not on the same page as you are theologically (or already on the defensive), how will a comparison be helpful? Again, this is a moment to listen.

Don't Try to Get Them Counseling

In this moment, another thing that some Christians will do is immediately suggest counseling. Now, the other person might, in fact, benefit from counseling. (In my opinion, all people need some kind of counseling.) But now is not the time to bring it up. This is not the moment to try to "fix" anyone; this is the moment to be a good friend, parent, sibling, or whatever your role may be with the other person. Just be there for the person.

In addition to those don'ts that you should always avoid when someone comes out to you, there is also a do that you shouldn't leave out.

Do Reaffirm Your Relationship

The other person may fear that by coming out he or she is going to jeopardize the relationship. Allay that fear at once. Say something like:

"My love for you is based on you, not your sexuality."

"This changes nothing about our relationship."

"God loves you no matter what, and so do I."

"I want our relationship to be a safe place where you can tell me anything."

Our reaction in the moment when someone comes out to us is a great example of acceptance without approval. It shows our love for them, and yet we have a chance to hold on to truth.

The Importance of "And"

I know there are those in the Christian community who want to clobber the LGBT community with verse after verse. Then there are those in the Christian community who will not consider hard verses and passages on this subject so that they can get along with everyone. Both sides sacrifice so much by not walking in the tension of grace and truth.

Rob Bell once stated, "God made some of us one way and some of us another, and it can be a beautiful thing." Bell added that the LGBT community are "our brothers. And you're our sisters. And we love you." He went on to talk about how we should embrace others, be kind, and recognize that we are all on a journey together. He finished by saying that we have to "do something about the truly big problems in our world." [10]

> Riding the tension between the two is much more demanding, but it is absolutely necessary.

I absolutely *love* the way that Bell loves people. I see the heart of Jesus in that kind of attitude and hope that I can be as loving. I don't, however, see evidence that God created some people to be gay. I'm not really concerned with the "Are people born that way" question. So what if they are? Even if someone were to find a "gay gene," I would still say it is a result of the fall of humanity recorded in Genesis 3. Yet I see many passages showing that God's standard for intimacy is between a man and a woman.

I'm much more concerned with a biblical worldview in regard to *this* issue rather than a birthright. Whichever side we land on with the whole "born that way" issue, we need to be careful.

My concern is when Bell—or anyone else—brushes aside the issue by saying that we have "real problems" to deal with. So, when God's Word says something is a sin that we need to deal with, do we just ignore that sin? Do we leave something alone that God says could interfere with our intimate relationship with him? Do we decide when not to deal with something or when a sin is no longer an issue? That seems to be glossing over what the Bible says about the Christian life.

The balance between grace and truth isn't an easy thing. If it were easy, we wouldn't have the issues we do. It's so easy to be on the side of grace (with no truth) or to be on the side of truth (with no grace). Riding the tension between the two is much more demanding, but it is absolutely necessary. It means there are times when you and I will side with grace on many issues,

> Another name for the tension between grace and truth is *love*.

but there are also times when we will side with truth. We will be people who are hard to figure out because accepting the tension between grace and truth is difficult and makes it look like we are on both sides. Actually, we *are* on both sides.

As I've said, another name for the tension between grace and truth is *love*. It's only when we accept the demands of living in this tension that we can show the fullness of love to people in the LGBT community (or anyone else who is different from us or is living far from God). The heavenly Father loves all his prodigal sons and daughters, among whom are you and me. He expects us to love others in the same way. This is the greatest love we could ever show another.

REFLECTION AND DISCUSSION QUESTIONS

1. Do you agree that there is a difference between acceptance and approval? What does this difference look like in your life?
2. Take some time to read the parable of the prodigal son (see Luke 15:11–32). What was the father's response to the prodigal son? Did the father have unconditional love or conditional love for his son? How does the father reflect God?
3. Do you think the older son was justified in behaving the way he did? Have you ever found yourself to be more like the older brother? How so?
4. Look at Romans 8:1, 31, 37–39. Identify the different aspects of God's love that these verses reveal. Is there any end to God's love for us? What does that say about God's love for those of us who struggle with various issues?
5. Now that you've read the first seven chapters of this book, answer this question: Why is the tension of grace and truth so messy?

Choose Your Relationship

It's much easier to get along with some in the LGBT community if you agree that sexuality doesn't have to be expressed just between a man and a woman. Believe me, I know how tempting it is to avoid the conflict and just go along with whatever the culture is promoting. Once you start talking about sexual expression only between a man and a woman, then naturally someone is going to get bent out of shape. The heat's going to come toward you.

What really hurts is when gay individuals you care about don't want anything more to do with you once they find out you believe that sexual intimacy is to be only between a man and a woman. Maybe you have a friend or family member who storms out of the room and out of your life after a discussion about homosexuality in which neither of you budges. Maybe you've been developing a friendship with an unbeliever who's gay, and once the topic of same-sex relationships comes up, *pffft*, the other person is gone and it seems as if all your relationship building was in vain.

It's hard.

But if a gay man or lesbian in your life essentially says, "Either you accept this part of my life or you leave me alone," then there can be only one right choice for you as a follower of Christ. You have to hold fast to what Scripture teaches on sexuality, regardless of the cost to your relationship with another person.

Now, I hasten to add that we shouldn't give up easily on our relationships with people who walk away from us. Sometimes a break with another person is not as permanent as it first seems. If we are patient and persistent and make it known that we're open for reconciliation, sometimes the other person comes back. We can always keep praying. And even if we lose a relationship with someone we care about, that doesn't mean we shouldn't keep pursuing others who need to know Jesus.

Immediately after I chose to follow Jesus, I found out how vulnerable relationships can be when the truth comes between people.

A Failing Grade

Silence. That was the sound in the room as I faced my father in his study. If you had been standing next to me in that moment, I think you could actually have heard the sound of my heart beating.

My dad and I just stared at each other.

Only minutes before, I had arrived home from being baptized and had walked up the stairs to Dad's study. He was grading papers when I entered the room, but he stopped as I sat down next to him. On the way home, I had concocted several schemes to tell him about my baptism, but in the end I just blurted out, "Dad, I got baptized!"

He didn't say anything. Dad just sat there staring at me.

Finally he broke the silence.

"You were raised Episcopalian! You were baptized and confirmed in the Episcopal Church!" His words were unyielding.

"Neither of those actions were my decision, Dad. Being baptized today and trusting Christ was a decision that I made free and clear of everyone else. I didn't do this as an insult to you or anyone else. I responded this way because I felt God wanted me to."

My dad's response was shaking his head, taking off his glasses, and setting them down next to the large stack of papers he'd been grading. Most of the papers were stained in red ink with his comments detailing how the student had messed up in the assignment. Right now, I felt like one of those students. I felt that in his eyes I had red ink all over me.

"You realize what you've done, right? You've spit in God's eye. You're saying your first baptism wasn't good enough."

My dad's words pierced my heart. How could I have spit in God's eyes?

"My decision today had nothing to do with my baptism as a baby. There was no way that I spit in God's eyes! I know that I made him happy today!" I retorted as my words gained more strength.

"Well, you haven't made me happy, and you're not going to make your mother happy," my dad shot back. He ended our exchange with grounding me for a few days.

At the time, I didn't know my dad was gay. Looking back now, I can easily see that he was worried I would reject him because he was secretly identifying as gay. For Dad, my baptism was basically a surface issue. On a deeper level, what was I going to start believing about his sexual orientation and behavior once I finally found out about them? This was what was driving his anger.

I didn't know any of that at the time, but I did know that my father had spoken the words I dreaded the most: "You're not going to make your mother happy."

It just so happened that in three days I was going to see my mother and Vera for the weekend. I decided to wait and tell them face to face about my new faith because it would be a more respectful way of breaking the news than talking to them over the phone, but it was not something I was looking forward to. In fact, for me as a sixteen-year-old, facing a monster from a horror movie would just about have been more enticing than having to share my decision with my mom.

It was a good thing Dad had grounded me. It meant I had time to read the Bible and prepare for the inevitable confrontation with my mother.

The Inquisition

A few days later, I got in the car with my dad and we drove halfway to my mom's house. Most of our trip passed in silence.

Finally my dad spoke. "Caleb, how are you going to tell your mom?"

Great question.

"I'm not sure."

"Well, you'd better figure it out because as much as you didn't like my reaction, you know that her reaction will not be fun either."

Not be fun either. Yep, that pretty much summed up my expectations for my weekend with my mom.

My dad and mom met at the McDonald's as usual, but this time we didn't even go in. Dad helped me put my things in Mom's car, looked at her, and said, "Have fun."

My mom shot him a puzzled look.

As we got in the car, she asked me, "What was he talking about?"

"Well, I've made some decisions," I started, "and I'm not sure you'll be thrilled about them."

Rolling her eyes, my mom whispered, "Oh no." She knew I'd

been attending some Bible studies, and I'm sure in that instant she had a pretty good idea of what I was going to say.

We had a ninety-minute car ride to her house, and every minute of it was awful. I told her all about my decision to follow Christ and the baptism I had undergone as a declaration of my new faith. To her, it was as if I had gone over to the enemy.

By the time we got home, my mom was in tears. She pulled into the garage, turned off the ignition, and stalked into the house. Vera heard her sobs and put her arm around Mom. Through the garage door window, I saw them talking. I was still sitting in the car and wasn't anxious to get out and take my medicine. I must have sat in the car for fifteen minutes.

When I at last came into the house, they were sitting next to each other in the living room. Not a word was spoken, but their expressions said everything. Disbelief, anger, and betrayal were some of the feelings playing across their faces.

"Sit down, Caleb," Vera invited.

I slowly walked into the living room and sat.

"So you're a Christian now?" she asked.

"Yes," I replied as I heard my mom whimper. "I am a Christian, but I still love you both and nothing has changed about that."

It was as if they hadn't heard my words at all.

"As a Christian, do you believe everything the Bible says?" Vera asked.

I paused, knowing I was getting ready to fall into a trap. "Yes," I said with little confidence.

Vera went on. "Okay, in the book of Revelation, when it says that a dragon is going to come out of the sea, do you believe that it will be a literal dragon?"

I began to sweat. I hadn't read Revelation yet. I didn't know the

interpretive rules of apocalyptic literature. I just knew that Jesus was
the Son of God. Taking a deep breath, I said, "If that's what the Bible
says, then yes."

Almost at the same time, my mom and Vera both began laughing at me.

"So, do you now believe that your mother and I are living in
sin?" Vera asked with a cynical look.

"Well, if the Bible says that—"

"I've heard enough! I'm going to bed," my mom shouted. She
headed toward the bedroom, with Vera following.

Before Vera entered the bedroom, she stopped and turned
around to glare at me. It actually felt as if she were staring right
through me. I was sitting on the couch in the living room, and I
wished the couch would swallow me up.

She shook her head and began by saying, "Do you realize the
amazing opportunity you have been given to be raised by two
women? Do you know that you are smarter than what you are becoming? Do you also know that you are siding with bigots?!"

I put my head down and softly said, "I'm not like that. I will
never be like that. I do not agree with your view of sexuality anymore, but that does not impact how much I love you."

"You'll change, Caleb," she retorted. "You'll eventually be like
the people you surround yourself with. The church you go to will say
a lot about who you will become and how you will treat people."
With that, she turned around and went into the bedroom, shutting
the door behind her.

The rest of the weekend went much like the initial conversation.
I felt as if I were being subjected to the Spanish Inquisition as my
mom and Vera quizzed me on issue after issue. I went home to my
dad's house emotionally bruised.

All this was good, in a way, because I became more determined than ever to know what the Bible says about a whole range of issues. Yet one thing was undeniable: a piece of the dream that my mom had for me died that weekend.

Accepting the Call

What happened next took me to a whole new level of being on the outs with Mom and Dad.

The next week, I went to a Christ in Youth conference in southern Missouri. I had never been to church camp or any kind of Christian conference before. This was a weeklong conference for high school students. Along with others from my youth group, I went to a local university, slept in a dorm, attended different classes during the mornings, participated in a small group during the week, and always went to an evening worship service with the speaker. I could not believe how awesome it was. I felt like I was in heaven. My friendships deepened and my faith grew, and I got to see that there were a lot of other high school students who were trying to live for God and were having difficult times.

At this conference, for some reason that I didn't understand, I quickly began to feel as if God was calling me into full-time vocational ministry. On Wednesday morning of the conference, I woke up and realized that I could do nothing else with the rest of my life than preach the gospel. This was one week to the day since I had been baptized. I knew God worked quickly—but I didn't expect him to work this quickly!

Each evening during the celebration worship service, the leaders would have an invitation time when you could give your life to Jesus for the first time, go forward for prayer, or go forward and dedicate your life to full-time vocational ministry. That Wednesday night, I went forward and gave my life to the ministry. I confessed before everyone that I wanted to be a preacher.

Soon afterward, I asked my pastor and some others where I could go to study for my newly determined career. They told me to consider going to Ozark Christian College in southern Missouri. That's all I needed to hear. I was sold on going to that school.

If you thought admitting to my parents that I was a Christian was a big deal, picture this: I was about to tell my university-professor parents that I was going to go to a small Bible college to train for ministry and would forgo applications to other universities.

I knew I couldn't put it off. The day I got home from the conference, I told the news to my dad in person and then I called my mother.

The carnage was much worse than before. The conversations and glares intensified.

One night, shortly after returning from the conference, I was walking up the stairs to my room, about to hit the hay. My dad walked to the bottom of the stairs and said, "Are you really going with this whole church thing?"

"Yes, Dad, I am," I responded. I was worn out by all these conversations.

"If you choose this route, Caleb, you're picking it over your mother and me," my dad declared.

"No, I'm not," I whispered to him so as to remain as calm as possible.

Then my dad pulled out this explosive statement: "If you choose to go this way, you are basically disowning your parents. How does that feel, Caleb?"

I was floored. Upset. Sad. Pick any emotion opposite to happy, and I probably was experiencing it in that moment.

"Dad, I don't even know how to respond to that," I firmly replied. "My love for God and my call to ministry don't change the way I feel about you. I love you and Mom, and that will never change."

My dad stormed off to bed and slammed his door.

My interactions were no better with Mom. She wrote my dad and me a long letter telling us that she would not pay for me to go to a Bible college. In this letter, she told me how disappointed she was about the decision I had made and that if I ended up going to a Bible college, I would not get a job and would probably wind up homeless on the streets.

The irony of this situation was that my parents thought I would disown them, when in actuality I felt as if they were disowning me.

When I think back on it, the reaction my parents had toward me "coming out" to them as a Christian and wanting to be a pastor was similar to what most heterosexual parents do when they discover their child is gay. It was the same amount of outrage and rejection. Except, in my case, the tables were turned. My parents were not upset because I was gay; my parents were upset because I was now Christian and they were gay!

There were a lot of things in Christianity that my parents didn't care for. But I think what hurt them most was that my new belief in the Bible forced me to deal with the issue of homosexuality and research what God's Word said about it. Obviously, the conclusion I came up with wasn't what they agreed with. It caused much friction between us. The hostility over the subject lasted for more than twenty years.

Loss and Reward

Sometimes when you are dedicated to God and you follow him, you lose relationships. Sometimes when you share the truth with people and it doesn't go over well, the relationship is never the same. Jesus talked about this after his encounter with the rich young ruler.

> God can never share devotion.

You remember that story, don't you? The rich young man comes up to Jesus and asks how to have eternal life—a seemingly perfect opening for Jesus to pull out his big black binder and start laying out the plan of salvation, as Gregg did with me. But Jesus spotted a hidden blockade in this guy's spirit: the young man was worshiping the idol of wealth. And God can never share devotion. So Jesus told the young man that he had to give away all his money.

The young man walked away disconsolate, still uncommitted to God.

Jesus, too, was grieving the outcome of the encounter. "How hard it is for the rich to enter the kingdom of God!" he exclaimed (Mark 10:23).

This stunned the disciples. They had grown up in a culture that said wealth was a sign of God's favor. So, how could wealth stand as a barrier to the kingdom of God?

Then Peter starting putting some things together. He said to Jesus, "We have left everything to follow you!" (verse 28). This was true. Although the disciples had not been as rich as the young ruler, they had given up their homes, their livelihoods, and, most of all, their families to follow Jesus.

Jesus acknowledged that people's decisions to follow him may cost them their nearest and dearest relationships. But he also gave assurance that it's worth it.

> "Truly I tell you," Jesus replied, "no one who has left home or brothers or sisters or mother or father or children or fields for me and the gospel will fail to receive a hundred times as much in this present age: homes, brothers, sisters, mothers, children and fields—along with persecutions—and in the age to come eternal life. But many who are first will be last, and the last first." (verses 29–31)

For me, this rings true.

When I say this was a hard season of my life, it really was. My relationship with my mother was the most important relationship I had. My relationship with my dad was also very important to me. When I was put in a position of having to choose either them or God, I was facing the most difficult decision of my life. Many nights I stayed up late and seriously thought about no longer following Jesus. If I did that, at least I would have my parents back.

I couldn't go back, though. Something had changed inside me. I had left the "old me" and was a "new me." God had transformed me into something different. And it was enough.

Jesus promises that if we choose him over any other relationship, he will bless us with persecutions (opportunities to stand up for him), but also we will have more relationships. I wasn't prepared for how true this was.

- I used to have no faith. Now I had plenty.
- I used to have no community. Now I had more friends than ever.

- I used to have no social life. Now I had a booming social calendar.
- I used to not know truth. Now I knew what was true and what wasn't.
- I used to have no mentor. Now I had several.
- I used to have no one to hold me accountable. Now I had people helping me.
- I used to be alone and dream about having relationships. Now it was reality.
- I used to be empty. Now I had God living inside me!

There may come opportunities in your life when you are able to tell people what God says about sexuality. They may not agree, and it may cost you your relationship with them. I want to give you encouragement for those moments. Don't give up! You have a God who hasn't given up on you. You have a Savior who died for you. God has promised you that he will reward you. And meanwhile, in the moments when you feel the most alone, he is very near.

> In the moments when you feel the most alone, God is very near.

I remember taking standardized tests in school. My classmates and I would go into the room, take out our Scantrons and number-two pencils, and begin taking the test. During this time, no one would talk, and our eyes were supposed to be on our own papers. Most of my standardized tests involved me picking the letter *C* over and over again. (I'm not good at standardized testing.)

But there was a consistent element in my tests: the teacher was always there. The teacher was silent, but he or she was always in the classroom, keeping watch over everything and hoping we would do our best on the test.

Now, I've heard this illustration before several times, but the principle is true! In the moments when you feel the most alone, God is there. After all, teachers are always silent during the tests, but they are still there. You might be going through a spiritual test right now and it may be making you feel that you are out on a limb alone, but God is there and he is cheering you on. Now is no time to give up. Faithfulness is always rewarded.

Pick the right relationship. Pick God.

God's Faithfulness to Rebuild

God slowly rebuilt my relationships with my parents and Vera. No matter what they said, I remained steadfast in my decision to go to Bible college. I would train to become a pastor, and this would never change how I felt about them—no matter what.

I did end up going to this college, and as amazing as it is, both of my parents helped me take out my first loan. I never thought that would happen, but they helped me get started at the college I wanted to go to. I would go back and visit my mom and dad at least once every other month. My mother was still active in the gay and lesbian community in Kansas City and was still involved in GLAAD, serving on the board of directors for the Kansas City chapter. I went with her to most of the parties and events she attended, and it provided a chance for me to build more relationships.

You, too, should keep on building your relationships with people in your life who aren't on the right path—even if you have tough conversations. Don't let rejection stop you. If you put him first, God will continue to do a good work through you, bringing blessing to you and blessing to those you care about.

REFLECTION AND DISCUSSION QUESTIONS

1. Have you ever lost a friend because you chose to do the right thing? What happened?

2. Why were Caleb's parents so threatened by him becoming a Christian? How do you think they felt when Caleb came out as a Christian? Why do you think they felt this way?

3. Read Mark 10:24–31. According to this passage, why is it so difficult when we follow Jesus? Has this happened in your life, or have you seen it manifested in the lives of others? How so?

4. Look again at Mark 10:24–31. What are the things God promises to give us when we follow him? How has this played out in your life?

5. Think about someone you've had to have a tough conversation with (or maybe someone had to have that conversation with you). How did God use that conversation? Has God healed that relationship? Do you expect God to do something with that relationship in the future?

Another Way

One thing I'm pretty sure we can all agree on is that God created us as sexual beings. Starting in the early pages of Genesis, the Bible is clear that God thought up sex (*Thank you, Lord!*) and encourages and blesses it in its proper context: marriage. I could, in fact, direct you to a few verses in the Song of Songs that get rather steamy. But even apart from what the Bible tells us, we all know from personal experience how powerful and how fundamental sexual desire can be in our lives.

I was definitely a sexual being at the time when I first came to Christ and began grappling with what my new faith meant for my views on sexuality and my relationships with my mom and Vera and their friends. Like most teenage boys, I was more than a little driven by my hormones. Interestingly, even though both my parents were gay, I never once experienced same-sex attraction. I often wondered if I would, but for whatever reason, it didn't happen.

But what if I *had* had homosexual feelings? And what about people who *are* gay or lesbian? What are they, as sexual beings, supposed to do with their desires?

This is a practical concern that all of us have to treat realistically as we develop relationships with people in the LGBT community.

Increasingly, in our own society and around the world, the accepted answer is gay marriage. "What's the big deal about two people of the same gender getting married?" many people (including Christians) ask today. "Why can't a couple get married if it isn't going to hurt anyone? Whose business is it whom somebody else loves or marries?"

I want to suggest that as people who are trying to hold on to grace and truth, we should encourage people to make choices about their sexuality that honor God. There are alternatives to same-sex relationships and gay marriage that can work for people today.

RSVP

The summer before I started attending Ozark Christian College, I tried to spend as much time with my family as possible because I knew my life was about to change dramatically. I spent about half the summer with my dad and half of it with my mom. My time with Mom included two fun weeks camping in Wisconsin with Vera's family.

One evening shortly after we returned to Kansas City from the camping trip, my mom came to my room with an invitation. "Caleb, two of our friends, Lynn and Jackie, have finally decided to get married! Vera and I are going. Why don't you come?" She told me when and where the event was to be held.

This was 1996 and gay marriage was illegal throughout the United States, but a lot of same-sex couples were holding wedding ceremonies anyway. In fact, I had been to several of these ceremonies, and although they had seemed boring to me (as any wedding would be), I had no objection to them. But as soon as Mom invited me to Lynn and Jackie's celebration, I began to feel uncomfortable inside.

If I went, this would be the first gay wedding I attended since becoming a follower of Jesus. And by now I had already gone a long way in learning that homosexuality is unbiblical. So I was pretty sure that a wedding ceremony between two women, even if it wasn't legal, was making the wrong kind of statement and setting up the wrong kind of relationship. If I went, would I be giving my implied blessing to something God did not approve of?

I hadn't worked this all out in my mind yet, but I was immediately hesitant about going to Jackie and Lynn's ceremony. At the same time, I didn't want my refusal to become a point of conflict in my relationship with my mom, which had recently begun to improve ever so slightly.

"Wow, I wish I could go," I said to Mom, "but I have to be back in Columbia during that time so I can do some church stuff."

That was true. It was also an excuse that allowed me not to wrestle with the tension I was feeling.

My mom had some inkling of the issues in my mind. "I don't think anyone will think any less of you if you do go, Caleb."

"I'm sure they wouldn't," I responded, "but I just can't go."

After I said that, my mom did what she normally did when she was mad at me—she went to her room and shut the door. Vera was already in there, sitting on the bed and reading a book.

At this point I did something that I wasn't used to doing: I tiptoed up to their bedroom door and pressed my ear against it. I can't overemphasize the fact that I didn't usually eavesdrop on my mom, but at this moment I was desperate to know what she was thinking.

Despite some muffled talk, I could make out a lot of their conversation.

"Vera, we are losing our son!" I heard my mom say. "He's not valuing what we value anymore. He's turning into this different person." She wasn't crying or worked up. She sounded defeated more than anything else.

"What do you expect?" Vera said to her. "I mean, have you seen the church he goes to? The books he's been reading? Why is this a surprise?"

Then Vera continued in a softer tone: "Caleb may be more Christian now than ever before, but he's still your son. He's still someone who loves you. He chose to be here for much of the summer. Doesn't that tell you anything?"

"It really bothers me," my mom said, "that my son doesn't agree with our relationship! It disturbs me that he thinks that something like a lesbian wedding is wrong. I'm finding that hard to move past."

I'd heard all I needed to. I stepped away from the bedroom door, crossed to my room, and turned on some music.

Sitting on my bed, I thought about what was going on. My investigation into what the Bible says about homosexuality had caused a great rift with my mom, dad, and Vera on one side and me on the other. Furthermore, my study of this subject had caused me to question one of the principles I had been taught my whole life: you are free to express your sexuality in any way you want.

I believe that was the first day when I really started considering what LGBT people should do with their desires for love and intimacy. If I was right that people like Jackie and Lynn shouldn't be getting married or having sex together at all, then how should they be living? What other options did they have for their sexuality and companionship needs?

I've wrestled with this issue much more over the years, and I've decided there's one option that people with same-sex attraction can always choose: celibacy. Yep, deciding to stay single and have no sex with anyone, period.

I know that the very suggestion that someone should never have sex can cause a strong reaction. (No sex, ever? *Gasp!*) In our sex-saturated culture, sex seems like a universal right, almost an obligation. Celibacy seems like an alien discipline that only a few people belonging to religious orders might, strangely, vow for themselves. Abstinence from sex seems unnatural and unrealistic, probably even cruel.

Through my reading of Scripture and my experiences with people who have chosen this option, however, I have come to look on celibacy as a beautiful possibility for people who are unable to fulfill their sexual desires in the ways that God has ordained in Scripture. In fact, sexual abstinence is what God expects of all people, whether heterosexual or homosexual, if they are not married to someone of the opposite sex. When chosen to honor God, celibacy can be holy and life-giving.

> Sexual abstinence is what God expects of all people, whether heterosexual or homosexual, if they are not married to someone of the opposite sex.

But before I get into specific reasons why I believe celibacy can be a positive thing for gay men and lesbians, I want to make sure that none of us takes this alternative lightly. We should never prescribe celibacy glibly. The truth is that the sexual feelings a person from the LGBT community has are just as powerful as those that anybody else has, and so it is no small thing when some choose to be celibate.[11]

If Our Places Were Switched

Play an imagination game with me. If you are married, think about your spouse. Or if you are not married, then for the sake of this exercise, imagine that you are.

Think back to the time when you were first getting to know the man or woman who would become your marriage partner. Remember the dates you went on, the long conversations you had, the yearning you experienced when you were apart. Recall the growing love you felt and how it lit up your life, turning your whole future rose-colored in your mind.

Now, for a moment, imagine that you were not allowed to marry this person or pursue any sort of intimate relationship with him or her. Even though you loved this individual more than anyone else in the world, you were not permitted to show the full measure of your love.

How would that make you feel?

Not so great, huh? That's putting it mildly, I know. My wife means the world to me, and I can't bear to think of the pain if we had been kept apart.

Well, there's more. Imagine that not only would you lose this relationship but also that you could never hope to find a similar one in the future. You could *never* marry someone, *never* know the companionship of a spouse, *never* let your sexual desires be fulfilled with a wife or husband, *never* have the "American dream" family life, *never* share your deepest thoughts and feelings in a relationship of complete openness. If you saw a pair of lovers holding hands and staring into each other's eyes, you would know that you could never have that experience. If you saw a sweet old couple completely at ease in each other's presence after decades together, you would know that you could never be like them.

Now how do you feel?

This illustrates for you what it feels like to LGBT people in a monogamous relationship when Christians ask them to give up their partner and be celibate. It's what it feels like to people who are gay when we tell them they can never be with someone of the same gender in a loving relationship. I cannot overemphasize what a tough situation this is for someone who identifies as LGBT. It might be the hardest decision they ever have to make—whichever decision they make about it.

As Christians, we need to be sensitive and understanding of the deep feelings that exist between two LGBT people. If they choose to surrender those feelings to God, it is a huge sacrifice. Let's respect that.

Nevertheless, since God designed sexual intimacy for a man and a woman, I believe celibacy is the right choice for people with same-sex attraction. In fact, it's not only the *right* choice, but it's a *good* choice for them, one they can embrace with gratitude.

Understanding the Gift

I know some people need convincing if they're going to look on celibacy as something that's good. I've heard single people say, "Caleb, please tell me why I should be happy about this gift, because I've been wanting to be with someone for a while." But I've been around long enough to notice that some people are single for a longer time than they wish and then get married later in life; some people never get married, without making peace with their state; and some people become so accustomed to living on their own that a partner would break up their way of life.

My point is, celibacy may actually prove to be a great thing for some people. It may be a gift from God.

The Gift of Celibacy According to Paul

To the Corinthians, Paul wrote, "I wish that all of you were as I am. But each of you has your own gift from God; one has this gift, another has that" (1 Corinthians 7:7). What is the gift he was alluding to?

If you ever go to seminary, one of the first things they'll teach you is that "context is king." In this case, context is a dictator! So when Paul said, "I wish that all of you were as I am," let's look at the context.

Paul had just finished discussing the sexual relationship between a husband and a wife:

> Now for the matters you wrote about: "It is good for a man not to have sexual relations with a woman." But since sexual immorality is occurring, each man should have sexual relations with his own wife, and each woman with her own husband. The husband should fulfill his marital duty to his wife, and likewise the wife to her husband. (verses 1–3)

So, when Paul said that he wished people would be like him (that is, have his gift), he was talking about celibacy. Paul himself was single, and he believed that singleness is a gift from God.

Why did Paul like being single so much that he wanted people to follow his example? Well, I think there are different blessings people get from being single.

One is freedom. Compared to married folks, people who are single often have more time to build relationships with others. They may have more freedom to do what they want with their life, to move wherever they want to live, and to focus on hobbies or talents. They may also have more opportunities to be generous, since they don't have to spend money on kids or a spouse. They live life without the particular stresses that marriage brings.

In addition, when people are single, they are able to focus more fully on the Lord. While I love being married, it does affect my priorities and my use of time. I have my focus on family first, then ministry, friends, personal projects, and other things. Singleness gives a celibate individual more time to focus on ministry in Jesus's name.

Paul understood this better than anyone else. Because Paul was on his own, he was able to travel, spread the gospel, mentor younger pastors, write theological letters, and do much more that shook up the Roman world for Jesus. Had he not been single, I'm not sure he would have had the opportunity to have such a sharp focus on God.

Paul, I'm convinced, got his respect for the potential of celibacy from his Lord, Jesus.

The Gift of Celibacy According to Jesus

In Matthew 19:1–12, we read about an encounter between Jesus and some Pharisees that spilled over into Jesus giving insights about celibacy to the disciples.

The Pharisees questioned Jesus about whether there is ever a good occasion for a man to divorce his wife. In his answer, Jesus reinforced God's original order for sexuality—the fact that God created the covenant of marriage between a man and a woman. In doing so, he quoted Genesis 1:27 and 2:24 as setting the precedent for intimacy within the male-female relationship. Using these verses, Jesus came down hard on divorce, even comparing some post-divorce remarriage to adultery.

The disciples, listening in, caught the seriousness of what Jesus was saying. They said to Jesus, "If this is the situation between a husband and wife, it is better not to marry" (verse 10). In other words, it is better to not marry at all than to violate what God has made one.

Here is where Jesus switched from discussing marriage and divorce to discussing celibacy. He replied to the disciples, "Not everyone can accept this word, but only those to whom it has been given. For there are eunuchs who were born that way, and there are eunuchs who have been made eunuchs by others—and there are those who choose to live like eunuchs for the sake of the kingdom of heaven. The one who can accept this should accept it" (verses 11–12).

This can be a little confusing. When Jesus said that some "choose to live like eunuchs," what did he mean? Was he saying that men should literally be castrated? Hardly. Consider the interpretation of New Testament scholar R. T. France:

> If to "make oneself a eunuch" is not to be understood
> literally . . . , it should probably be understood along the lines
> of some modern versions, "to renounce marriage" (NIV, REB),
> "do not marry" (GNB). The first two categories were inca-
> pable of marriage; this third group represents those who have
> voluntarily chosen celibacy. Their choice is ascribed not to
> disinclination but to their perception of God's will for them:
> the "kingship of heaven" means God's sovereign authority,
> and it is in obedience to that authority that they have been
> prepared to stand apart from the normal expectation of
> marriage and fatherhood. The phrase does not in itself
> indicate what is the specific purpose for which God may have
> called and enabled such people to be celibate. It does not
> denote specifically, for example, either an overriding impera-
> tive of evangelism or the call to a contemplative life. These
> and other reasons may explain God's call in certain cases, but
> Jesus' statement here is much more general: some are celibate
> because they believe this to be God's will for them.[12]

So there are some who are called to celibacy and choose to ac-cept what God has given them. As seriously as Jesus took marriage (because God is the author of marriage), Jesus took celibacy just as seriously. Jesus, like Paul, described celibacy as a gift. He ended his speech on the matter by saying that whoever can accept this gift should accept it.

On the basis of these words from Paul and Jesus, I unhesitatingly affirm that celibacy is a gift that God has for some.

Also, consider the following people who were single (to the best of our knowledge): Miriam, Elijah, Elisha, Jeremiah, Daniel, Nehemiah, Anna, Martha, John the Baptist, Mary Magdalene, Paul, Barnabas, Timothy, Lydia, John, and probably some of the other disciples. These were some of the most faithful and effective people for God in Bible times. And I'm sure that if we were to investigate the lives of other people in the pages of the Bible, we would find even more who were celibate during their whole life or a substantial portion of their adulthood.

Biblically speaking, celibacy isn't some kind of abnormality but rather is truly a gift God has made available to people for various reasons.

Celebrating Celibacy

If you experience same-sex temptations, or if you are a friend to someone who does, then it's important to look at what celibacy really means. It *doesn't* mean living as a hermit and feeling lonely all the time. Certainly there often *is* loneliness in celibacy, but how much and how it affects celibate people is up to them. Celibacy offers an alternative to marriage that is full of good things in its own way.

Consider the following three perspectives on celibacy.

Celibacy Honors the Truth About Celibates
While Acknowledging What They Believe

For those who have same-sex feelings and yet accept that sexual intimacy is to be expressed only between a man and a woman, celibacy is profoundly honest.

First of all, through celibacy, they acknowledge the feelings they have. It's like saying, "I'm alone and not in a relationship with a member of the opposite sex because I don't have those kinds of feelings. Like it or not, I have feelings for people of my own gender."

At the same time, in celibacy, they are saying that they want to hold true to what the Bible says about sexuality. Their meaning is "I'm not in a relationship with a person of my own gender because I realize that would be wrong in God's eyes. And God is more important to me than any selfish fulfillment of my own desires."

Celibacy Is an Example to Others

Celibate people show the world that Jesus is enough for them. They become living examples of how Jesus can fulfill any person, no matter their life situation.

More specifically, celibacy can actually be a tool to help spread the gospel. Let me explain what I mean by telling you a true story.

A man named Steve* started attending the church that my friend Matt pastored. Steve was gay. When he encountered some marketing materials that celebrated the church's diversity, he assumed that meant the church endorsed people in openly gay and lesbian relationships. That's why he decided to check out this particular church.

During the first few weeks of attending Matt's church, Steve was inspired by the stories of gospel-driven life transformation from

---

* This name has been changed.

Scripture and from people in the church. He called on the name of Jesus for salvation, confessed Christ as Lord, and was baptized. He wasn't sure if he believed all of Scripture, especially the parts about homosexuality, but he still wanted to follow Jesus and be a part of the community of believers.

Months passed, during which Steve was both a Christian and a gay man living as he had before.

Then one Sunday, in a sermon, Matt made the point that if the Bible is true, we have to accept what it teaches about sin, however inconvenient or uncomfortable that might be for us. In this sermon Matt did not mention homosexuality in particular, yet Steve began to feel convicted by the Holy Spirit about his sexuality. He struggled for a while, then finally submitted to what he knew God was calling him to. He chose to become celibate rather than express his sexuality with other men.

You might think that at this point Steve separated from the LGBT community. No. He did something more courageous—and more influential—than that. He used his celibacy as a witness to the power of the gospel in his life, having many conversations about God with his LGBT friends. A number of these friends accompanied him to church, and they, too, learned about the transformation Jesus offers.

Celibacy Doesn't Have to Equal Loneliness

Although many people avoid celibacy because they fear loneliness, I have seen that this fear is exaggerated. No one who follows Jesus is ever really alone. Jesus promises as much in Matthew 28:20: "Surely I am with you always, to the very end of the age." Moreover, in John 14:16–17, he explains that God himself will take up residence within us in the form of the Holy Spirit. This means followers of Jesus are never on their own, even if they have no sexually intimate relationships.

From a practical standpoint, people who have chosen celibacy don't have to live alone if they don't want to. I know many LGBT people who are celibate and who have richer lives because they have roommates, live with families, or even find comfort in living on their own. I know that a friend will never be a replacement for a spouse, but sharing living space with others can be an alternative to living alone. In fact, it can provide some deep and lasting relationships.

Celibacy is a beautiful tradition in the Christian church, going back to our founder and Lord, the unmarried Jesus. No one needs to consider the prospect of celibacy with horror. God can use it for good in the lives of many people. This is why we can present celibacy as a valid option and desirable possibility for people with same-sex attraction who want to honor God's commands.

And by the way, celibacy doesn't have to be a lifelong situation. For some there is still another option.

The Redemption of Marriage

During my college years, I had several internships as a preacher. (I will tell more about this in the next chapter.) One couple I met during one of these internships was Jerry and Betty.* When I first encountered Jerry, I immediately wondered if he was gay. He didn't have any giveaway mannerisms, but I still had my suspicions, which I kept to myself.

One day this couple took me to lunch. Now, there are two things you need to know if you are considering becoming a pastor.

---

* These names have been changed.

First, many people will want to take you out to eat. You have a strong chance of gaining weight! Second, when people take you out, they will eventually want to tell you their life story. I don't know if it is out of an instinct for confession, authenticity, wanting to impress you, needing advice, or a blend of all these, but people have a way of spilling their guts to preachers. In my lunch appointment with Jerry and Betty, it didn't take long for them to launch into their life story.

Guess what? I was right—Jerry was gay. It confirmed to me again that after being raised in the LGBT community, I was pretty good at figuring out this sort of thing.

Speaking freely before me and his wife, Jerry said he couldn't remember when he didn't feel attracted to other men. But Jerry had been raised in a Christian home, knew the Bible from an early age, and believed that his sexual feelings weren't what God wanted for him. So he resisted temptations to pursue intimacy with other men.

Jerry next went on to tell me about his marriage. He and Betty met when she started working in the company where Jerry was employed. They discovered that they had a lot in common and immediately became friends. Over time, they developed deep feelings for each other and got married. By the time I met them, they had been married for several years and had three kids.

This tale, simple as it was, was fascinating to me, and I had to explore further. "But how could you get married to a woman if you were attracted to men?" I asked.

Jerry's answer shocked me. He said, "I married Betty because she was my best friend. I truly believed that marriage could be a redemptive place for my feelings—and it was."

Wow! I hadn't even considered that possibility. A loving heterosexual marriage could redeem same-sex feelings.

I continued to ask questions of both of them, eager to understand how their relationship worked. I found out that even though Jerry was attracted to his wife, he still was attracted to other men too.

"But how are you able to stay married and faithful to Betty if you still have these feelings?" I asked Jerry.

Both of them chimed in at this point. And as they talked, I began to get a picture of the values that helped them keep their relationship solid.

First, honesty was essential. Betty knew that Jerry still had these feelings and that he couldn't just shut them off. In return, Jerry knew that he had to be honest about his feelings and let Betty know when he was struggling. This required constant communication with each other. They had to always be talking and always be willing to understand how the other was feeling.

Next, to handle feelings that they had as a result of their unique relationship, they prayed a lot. In fact, their prayer life with each other (and individually) was amazing. They were in the habit of praying daily for the other person and asking God to give them peace and grace.

You know what that resulted in? They became incredibly close with each other. In fact, far from their unusual marriage not working (as we might expect), they were *closer* than the average married couple.

Their relationship had its foundation in honesty, communication, and prayer. It resulted in holy living and a happy family. I could see now why Jerry called his marriage redemptive.

Please hear me on this: I'm not saying that everyone who is gay should go out and find a spouse of the opposite sex. Probably for most people who have same-sex attraction and want to honor God, celibacy is the more viable option. Still, some LGBT people shouldn't discount marriage with a member of the opposite sex. It may become possible at some point.

If they feel God is calling them to such a marriage, they can trust him to be faithful to bring it about and help them in the midst of it. The rest of us in the body of Christ can be supportive and encouraging for those who choose heterosexual marriage despite their same-sex feelings. If they're like Jerry and Betty, they'll be doing a lot of praying. We should be praying with and for them.

How to Approach the Choice

I want to do something different now and address my gay and lesbian readers specifically. If that includes you, read on. If not, feel free to skip this section of the chapter—or stick with me and keep learning.

If you are LGBT, you may be thinking, *I didn't agree with the chapter on what the Bible says about homosexuality, and I certainly don't agree with this chapter.* You might have a same-sex partner, be in love with someone of the same sex, or dream of being with someone of the same gender, and the ideas of celibacy and heterosexual marriage just seem unreasonable to you. Maybe you're even a little mad at me at this point and want to throw the book away.

I can accept that. But if you're willing to hang with me longer, and if you're willing to at least consider celibacy, then I have a few things I want to share with you about how to make the decision.

Put God's Call Above Your Own Preference
While salvation is a free gift, living for Jesus still calls for sacrifice. Jesus asks us all to give up things for him. That's the point of the

story of the rich young ruler, which I brought up in the last chapter. Sometimes what we have to sacrifice seems like more than we can bear to give. But if God asks us to make a sacrifice, he will also give us the grace to obey.

So, when I say that you should put God's call above your personal preferences, I'm not asking you to do anything fundamentally different from what any other Christian would have to do. If you truly believe that sexuality, as God designed it, is to be between a man and a woman, then you should be willing to give up what he asks of you. Here is where your faith goes into action.

> Living for Jesus still calls for sacrifice.

Don't Base Your Decision on Feelings Alone

Feelings are important. Emotions are necessary. We need to pay attention to them. Here's the thing, though: feelings are some of the most deceptive tools in our life. The Bible drives this point home several times in verses such as Jeremiah 17:9:

> The heart is deceitful above all things
>   and beyond cure.
>   Who can understand it?

I lie to myself about myself a lot. I'm sure you do too. Sometimes you think too lowly of yourself, believe horrible things others say about you, and can't imagine that you are the subject of God's lavish love. All of this contradicts who you really are, but it *feels* true in the moment, and those feelings can mislead you.

In the same way, our feelings about love and intimacy can lead us astray.

I'm not saying that your feelings of love for another person are imaginary, because they're not. Those emotions are real. My point is that our feelings on a matter sometimes are the greatest drive to why we believe what we believe.

This shouldn't be the case. The Bible should be the reason we believe what we do. Feelings change, but God's Word never changes. It is always consistent. So if the Bible teaches that an intimate relationship between two people of the same gender is wrong, that has to trump your same-sex feelings of attraction for a person, however strong and persistent those feelings may be.

> The Bible should be the reason we believe what we do. Feelings change, but God's Word never changes.

Be Gracious in Your Decision, Whatever It Is

If you end up coming to the conclusion that Scripture allows for same-sex relationships, then please remember that those who don't agree with you are entitled to their opinion too. Many people have studied the Bible texts and decided that marriage is defined between a man and a woman, and they aren't homophobic or any less loving because of it. Don't shut people out of your life because they don't see eye to eye with you or the person you're in a relationship with. *Don't do to others who disagree with you what you would be afraid of them doing to you.*

On the other hand, if you come to the conclusion that homosexuality is not what God designed for sexuality, then you should also be gracious to those who disagree. Understand that this was probably not an easy decision for some, and it shouldn't affect how you treat or love them. You can hold to your beliefs and still love these people.

Celibate gay Christians, just like celibate straight Christians, need to keep showing grace to people who openly live in and affirm same-sex relationships.

Love, Sex, and Marriage in the Real World

Before I finish this chapter's subject, I want to come back around to the particular issue that got me started thinking about what people in the LGBT community should do with their sexual feelings: attending a same-sex wedding.

This is one of the most common questions I get: "My friend or family member is LGBT and is getting married. Should I go to the wedding?"

My thinking on this has advanced since I first declined to attend Jackie and Lynn's ceremony with my mom. I tell people that they have two options when they are invited to a same-sex wedding.

The first is to attend if they want to. This will place them in a difficult situation as a follower of Jesus, but they will gain influence with the relationship, will be seen as someone who is loving, and might get a chance to witness to people at the wedding. Also, the couple might call on them later when they get into a difficult situation—and that will give them a chance to speak truth.

The other option is not to attend. While it may hurt the feelings of the couple getting married, it's a way of standing up for the truth that marriage is a covenant between God and an opposite-sex couple. He has standards for sexual intimacy, and some people don't want to be in a position where it looks like they are supporting or approving of something that God says not to.

In either decision, it will be hard, and that is how we walk the tension between grace and truth. We wrestle between the two.

We can encourage celibacy or heterosexual marriage for our friends with same-sex attraction. But in the end, the choice will be theirs. What's not up for debate is how we treat people. We must keep loving them regardless of their decision, representing God's grace and truth as well as we know how.

Stories of people like Steve, who chose celibacy, and Jerry, who made a heterosexual marriage work with the help of a wonderful wife, may be rare. But they belie the common claim that giving in to same-sex feelings is the only realistic or desirable option. I believe that when people honor the way that God created the sexes, he *always* blesses that.

Now, as we continue on this journey, I want to broaden the discussion and talk about not just what you can do as an individual but also how your church relates to people in the LGBT community. What I have to say may make some church leaders uncomfortable, but I believe it's a message that can transform the relationship between the Christian community and the LGBT community.

REFLECTION AND DISCUSSION QUESTIONS

1. Have you ever been asked to attend a same-sex wedding? What was your reaction? What is your vision of gay marriage?
2. What do you believe about celibacy? Is this a realistic option for people who are gay? Why or why not?
3. Do you believe that the covenant of marriage is redemptive? How have you seen redemption occur in your marriage or the marriage of others? Is it realistic to believe that sexuality can be redeemed in marriage?

4. Read John 14:15–27; 15:26–27; and 16:7–15. How do you see the Holy Spirit leading and guiding you in life? How is God always with us through his Spirit? Is it fair to say that we are never spiritually alone?

5. How can we be gracious and loving with those who disagree with us? How can we be gracious toward those with whom we disagree?

A Messy Church

Think about your church and ask yourself if it's a place where it's okay for people to say things like these:

- "I'm an addict and I want to know my next step."
- "I can't handle my finances."
- "I'm struggling with porn."
- "I'm not doing well in my marriage."
- "I gossip and feel better when I run people down."
- "I'm having issues with my kids."
- "I'm struggling with my sexuality."
- "I'm gay."

I list these topics because so many people have talked to me about them, and then they say things like "I would never bring this up at my church" or "I want to talk to you because I can't talk to my pastor about this" or "The people in my small group would never understand."

I don't know about you, but I've been a part of more than one church where you didn't want to get your hand caught in the cookie jar. If you did, you would be disciplined in a way that had no compassion and you would feel humiliated. The lesson was clear: don't air your dirty laundry to others in church.

Hear me on this. The church should be the *first* place someone would go for conversations like these. Yet for many it's the *last* place. Why in the world would anyone go to a group of people who would make them feel guilty and worse for what they are struggling with? Instead of going to church, they will go to other places to share their struggles and feelings—and a lot of those places are not good. Or if they do go to church and just keep their secret to themselves, they don't heal, because nobody can heal from something they don't own.

It's a sad state.

But I do have hope. I have hope because it seems like there are more and more churches where "it's okay not to be okay," as my friend Jud Wilhite says. At such churches, you can show up and discover an expectation that you're just as messed up as the next person. You can be honest about your struggles and your past because it's in the DNA of these churches for people to be real.

> I want you to become a change agent, moving the culture of your local church in the direction of more openness toward people who are different from you.

When you find a group of believers like this, they won't expect you to be perfect. They will give you room to work out the struggles between you and God. They don't view themselves as God's moral security team but instead are more than happy to walk alongside you in the journey. If it gets confusing sometimes when they try to show both grace and truth, well, that's the way it goes. You'll have to live in the tension, just like they will.

I call this kind of church a *messy church,* and I want to enlist you in the messy church movement.

I want you to become a change agent, moving the culture of

your church in the direction of more openness toward people who are different from you. Even if you're not a pastor or other leader in the church, you have a voice and you can speak up for changes in policies and attitudes to welcome those who are struggling with sin problems while they are searching for God. Change may happen slowly and bit by bit in your church, but if you and other like-minded people in your congregation keep the pressure on, it has to happen eventually.

> If our churches are places where people can't be honest, we are creating sanctuaries for fake people.

If we get this wrong, our churches will become places that are messy in a bad way, not a good way. Because if our churches are places where people can't be honest, we are creating sanctuaries for fake people. Ultimately, our churches become Pharisee factories.

Early in my career, I found to my disgust that I was actually the pastor of one such Pharisee factory.

The Education of a Student Preacher

When I started attending Ozark Christian College in 1996, it was my first time being around so many Christians at once. I loved being in the dorms. I loved making new friends. I loved living in a place where everybody seemed to love Jesus in the same way I did. For me as an extrovert, it was a dream come true. There was always something going on—some event to attend, students hanging out, groups studying Scripture, or whatever. I never had a dull moment in college.

College was also how I got launched into church ministry, fulfilling the commitment I had made at the youth conference a week after beginning to follow Jesus.

Not long after starting at Ozark, I heard that students could go to churches and preach on the weekends if a certain church needed a preacher. I signed up as quickly as I could because I wanted to preach. I had not had one preaching class or even finished my first semester of college, and yet I was already volunteering to go out and preach if any church needed a preacher.

The first church I preached for had six people. The youngest member was seventy years old. They wanted me to stay and be their preacher and start a youth group. I suppose we could have had a youth group of forty-year-olds.

Other churches I went to had different personalities. I remember one in particular, which was a whole family meeting in a building. I got up to preach, and they started a family argument right in the middle of my sermon. I actually had to stop my sermon and shush them. I'm proud to say that I've never had to do that since.

Finally I found a church that I liked, and I ended up staying for eighteen months. It met in a small town an hour's drive north of the college. The town had fifty residents, twenty-five of whom were members of the church. I guess you could say that at that time we were the largest church per capita of any town in the world!

The church building was a white wooden structure right in the center of town. The inside of the church was old and dusty. The hymnals were falling apart. The numbers on the attendance board were left over from at least fifteen years earlier. The entire building consisted of a medium-sized room with wooden pews and a back room where you could have Sunday school or children's ministry. Unfortunately, there were no children in the town, so we had no children's ministry.

The people who attended this church were farmers or owners of small shops. All of them had been going to that church for a while and knew each other very well. When I started preaching there, I was the only one who did not know anyone.

A couple of things made this first pastoral experience difficult for me.

First, I was not used to preparing a sermon every week. Prior to this, I would be called maybe once or twice a month to preach at an area church. When I agreed to preach at this church, however, I had to come up with the sermon every single week, and as a full-time student, I couldn't always seem to get around to it.

One Sunday I didn't have a sermon, so I brought a commentary on the gospel of John with me to church. This is funny (and a little shameful at the same time), but I got up and read half of the first chapter of the commentary to the congregation. What was even more amusing was that they didn't care. They thanked me afterward for informing them on the textual issues in John 1!

The second thing that made this ministry difficult was that we did not have good music. I mean, I know that God loves it when his children praise him, but I think God may have made an exception for our church. We had twenty-five people who had no idea how to hit a note.

What was even funnier was that we didn't have anyone to play the piano, just a woman who had absolutely no idea what to do with it. She would sit down at the piano every Sunday morning and start banging her fingers on the keyboard. There was no rhyme or reason as to why she hit the notes that she did. No one ever put up a fuss about it, and everyone just kept on singing as if she were doing a brilliant job.

For eighteen months, I preached there Sunday after Sunday, performed hospital calls, visited people on their birthdays, and did so much more.

One other thing that I kept on trying to do was to convince my mother to come to church with me. Since I had become a Christian, she had not yet made a commitment to go to church with me, even though I had begged her. Getting Vera to come was definitely never going to happen, but finally my mother agreed to come. I was so excited! I was proud to preach before her, and I hoped the experience would be a step in moving her toward Jesus.

I picked her up early the next Sunday morning and we drove to the church together. When we walked up the old, creaky steps of the building and opened the door, I don't think any of the church members inside knew what to do. I had talked about my mom in my sermons, so they knew who the woman with me was and the fact that she was a lesbian, and now they just stared at her. Finally a couple came over and greeted her pleasantly, but afterward they walked away as fast as they could.

Then the singing started. My mother has a great sense of humor, and she laughed during the entire worship time. She tried to keep it to herself, and fortunately it's possible that no one heard her laugh because of how loud and bad the singing was.

After that, I got up to preach, completed the service, and finally said good-bye to the congregation until the next week. Then I headed home with Mom.

In the car I asked her what she thought about the service.

She said she had enjoyed herself. She also said she had not laughed that hard in a long time and would definitely not be coming back anytime soon.

Well, at least I got her to come to church, right?

The next Sunday I pulled up to the church, only to find two elders waiting for me at the front door of the building. As I walked up the steps, I got a feeling like I was in trouble. One of the men asked me to come to the back room with them.

Once we had slipped into the back room together, one of the elders said, "If you ever want to preach at this church, don't you ever bring anyone else like that again!"

I won't ever forget those words. I was in shock. I had spent the last year and a half preaching to, investing in, and trying to help these people understand how the gospel is for everyone, and now they did not want somebody who was far away from Jesus to attend their church.

My response was curt: "Excuse you?"

"We are not a church that accepts those kinds of people!" the leader said back to me. Talk about an us-versus-them mentality.

"Well, consider this my last Sunday," I said as I verbally handed in my resignation. "As a matter of fact, I don't need to preach today."

"What? No, you need to preach today, and you can stay, but things need to change," the other elder pleaded.

"Nope," I said. "I'm done. But I'll preach today."

I rolled up my sleeves and gave this group the harshest sermon I could on evangelism and the gospel. After I was done, I grabbed my notes and my Bible, walked down the center aisle while they were doing their invitation song, got in my car, and drove away forever.

Today, as I look back, I can see that I didn't handle the situation in the best possible way. Even in the face of ugliness, we should be full of grace. At the time, though, I was young and sure of myself (don't Bible college and seminary students know everything?), and so I reacted instinctually. But do you know what? Even if my reaction wasn't entirely what it should have been, my anger was totally justified. I think the hardheartedness of those church elders must have reminded Jesus watching from up in heaven of the attitudes he encountered among the Pharisees.

To this day, I have not returned to see what happened to that church. Maybe one day I will. I hope they are different.

That was when I decided that I never wanted to preach at a church like that again. I told myself that whenever I got to lead my own church, I wanted a church that was filled with alcoholics, drug users, gang members, people who are bankrupt, people who have no jobs, people who are having marriage issues, people who are struggling with their sexuality, people who are gay, people who are having affairs, people who are depressed, people who are gossipers, even people who are angry church members, because that is the church Jesus lived for, bled for, died for, rose for, and is coming back for!

> Jesus did not die on the cross to create a little country club.

Jesus did not die on the cross to create a little country club where we could have weekly gatherings, pat ourselves on the back for our good behavior (while hiding our bad behavior), and meet in clusters during the week but do nothing to reach out to the community. That's not the kind of church Jesus wants built here on earth.

The Perfect Church

If you could picture the perfect church, what would it look like? Who would be the pastor? Who would attend? Who would be the members? What would be required for membership? How would the people be dressed?

Well, you know what they say: If you find the perfect church, don't join it. You'll ruin it!

Jesus told a parable that can help us think about who should be in our churches. This parable describes two different types of people. These were everyday people in Jesus's day, and truthfully, they are everyday people in our day as well. Here is the parable in full:

> Two men went up to the temple to pray, one a Pharisee and the other a tax collector. The Pharisee stood by himself and prayed: "God, I thank you that I am not like other people—robbers, evildoers, adulterers—or even like this tax collector. I fast twice a week and give a tenth of all I get."
>
> But the tax collector stood at a distance. He would not even look up to heaven, but beat his breast and said, "God, have mercy on me, a sinner."
>
> I tell you that this man, rather than the other, went home justified before God. For all those who exalt themselves will be humbled, and those who humble themselves will be exalted. (Luke 18:10–14)

Short and sweet. I like parables like this.

As you keep the parable in mind, think about what you and I probably have in common with the Pharisee:

- We both believe the Hebrew Scriptures are divinely inspired.
- We both believe in the Resurrection and in a Messiah.
- We both believe in the importance of living a life pleasing to God.
- We both believe we need to share the truth about God.
- We both believe we need to practice spiritual disciplines such as prayer and fasting.
- We both believe in angels, demons, heaven, and more.

- We both believe in studying God's Word and knowing it well.
- We both believe in teaching other people about God.

You and I have more in common with the Pharisee than we usually assume, don't we?

The thing that scares me is that in a lot of churches in America, many Christians would feel more comfortable with having the Pharisee in their church than with having the person who is currently involved in sin or has a wretched past.

At first glance, the tax collector seems like he is *not* like us at all. Looking deeper inside the tax collector, though, we might find more of ourselves there than we do in the Pharisee. We also might find that the tax collector is actually spiritually deeper than the Pharisee. Here's what I see in the tax collector:

- He loves God.
- He acknowledges that he fails God.
- He calls himself a sinner.
- He owns his junk.
- His sin is causing him emotional and physical pain.
- He admits to doing things that God says not to.
- He struggles with sadness over his sin.
- He understands that his life depends on God's mercy.
- He is so humble that he doesn't make a show of his prayer.
- He doesn't feel worthy on his own to approach God.

When I first became a Christian, I was able to relate to the tax collector easily. As time went on, though, I became more and more able to understand the Pharisee, and the tax collector seemed like more of a stranger. How about you?

I believe all of us have to fight a legalistic, insider spiritual gravitational pull so that we do not become the Pharisee. We need to hold on to the traits of the tax collector. We also need to resist some of the traits of the Pharisee I didn't mention—traits like thinking we're more spiritually advanced than we really are, forgetting what sins we're responsible for and how desperately we need forgiveness, focusing on secondary issues, trying to force other people to have the same priorities we do, and refusing to have anything to do with messy people. This

> The tax collector is actually spiritually deeper than the Pharisee.

is a battle we will fight for the rest of our lives, and we ought to be helping others fight the same battle.

For me, the perfect church would be a church with more "tax collectors" and fewer religious people. When you have a church that is made up of less-than-perfect people, you'll have a *messy church.* And the crazy thing is, messiness begets more messiness. In other words, if you have a messy church, you'll have a church that will grow and expand because it will attract even more less-than-perfect people.

I wish the little church I pastored in college had been a messy church. I wish all churches were messy churches, because then we could feel comfortable about inviting friends and family from the LGBT community to worship and study with us. We wouldn't have to fear that they would be hurt and rejected. Along with all the other less-than-perfect people (ourselves, for instance), they would be in a place where they could have their hearts softened toward God in the presence of God's people. That's the power of a messy church.

And a messy church reflects a gospel that can look messy.

The Messy Gospel

I believe the gospel of Jesus Christ is messy. I'm not insulting the gospel. It isn't messy actually, but it *looks* messy when it goes to work in messy lives.

The gospel looks messy because it can lead to lives becoming harder, not easier. We are called to love and reach the same kinds of people Jesus did—and that will always be met with criticism. When you look at the people Jesus hung out with and how he was mocked for hanging out with those people, you have to understand that you and I will get the same treatment to some degree, not only from the world, but also from our religious brothers and sisters.

The gospel of Jesus Christ is worth whatever mess it may seem to cause, because it changes lives. It is the only source in existence that changes lives for the better and keeps them better. It is the only gift that gives us eternal life, but there is also no other call that sends us out to other people like the gospel. When we look at how the gospel has changed lives, it is phenomenal.

- A crucified criminal replaced a hard heart with a change of heart.
- Peter changed from a denier of the Lord to a preacher.
- Paul transformed from a persecutor to a missionary.
- Priscilla became a disciple after being an ordinary citizen.
- Matthew turned from a tax collector to a biblical author.
- Timothy grew from a timid young man to an effective pastor.
- Thomas reversed his attitude from doubt to faith.

- Mark exchanged being a quitter to being a useful asset to Paul's ministry.
- Mary Magdalene was moved from a wanderer to a Jesus follower.
- James switched from being an unbelieving brother of Jesus to the head of a church.
- John was an angry guy wanting to call down fire, but then he saw heaven itself.

When you have people who have dramatic shifts like these individuals did, then you need to watch out! There is a strong movement on the rise, and the cause will spread to the world like wildfire.

As awesome as it probably was to live in the first century and see the early church grow, I think we have even more of a chance to see a revival in our day. More than ever, the church in America has a chance to make a huge impact, but it all starts with who makes up our church and who we believe in. Obviously, we all believe in God and believe that it is his church, not our church. When we have a church filled with religious zealots and Pharisees, however, it becomes hard to host the kind of transformation that the early church saw.

> The gospel of Jesus Christ is worth whatever mess it may seem to cause, because it changes lives.

Every single person in the list you just read had major issues in his or her life. Most of the biblical leaders we read about in the Bible made huge mistakes, and yet for some reason God still used them. In many cases, it was their worst mistake that led to their greatest victory.

The same is true today.

If we have a church filled with people who are honest and vulnerable about their shortcomings, then the gospel will know no boundaries. When people have the past of the tax collector and they have experienced grace, they're able to communicate grace, love, and truth in a way that many people are not able to explain.

Everything I said in earlier chapters about personally showing grace and truth to people in the LGBT community is crucial. But if we don't have *churches* that also know how to show grace and truth, we'll never fundamentally overcome the hostility between the Christian community and the LGBT community. Gay and lesbian people like my mom, Vera, and my dad will continue to feel shut out of the very congregations where they ought to be welcomed and kept safe as they learn to know and follow Jesus. Following the gospel can make ours a messy church like this.

As I think back to that old country church where I preached when I was in Bible college, I realize that it wasn't a messy church. It was a church that had forgotten whose it was and what its mission was. It was a church that had potential but was too afraid of people who were different. Unfortunately, it was a church that was more comfortable with the apparent uprightness of a Pharisee than the messiness a tax collector would bring.

God desires for us to be messy. The mission is too important not to be.

What a Messy Church Looks Like

So, how can you tell you're in a church that is messy? What does it look like to be in a church that embraces the tension of grace and truth and understands the struggle that many in the LGBT community have?

In my view, a good church is one that is willing to talk about any and every scenario. In our culture, churches need to know where they stand and the leadership needs to be unified. I want to give you some example questions that illustrate some very real scenarios you will eventually face at your church, if you haven't already. Some of these questions may be

> Church needs to be a place where you can "belong before you believe."

hard for you to consider. Other questions might yield easy answers. Regardless, my goal here is not to assume an answer to any of these questions. My hope is that more churches will allow themselves to have conversations they haven't had in the past.

Here are some questions for you and your church to answer:

- Would you allow a same-sex couple to attend your church?
- What would the reaction be if two men were holding hands in the lobby of your building?
- Could a lesbian couple who attend your church also attend a parenting class that you're putting on (because their child is in your children's ministry)?
- Could an LGBT couple attend a community group or Bible study?
- Could an LGBT couple serve anywhere in your church? If so, where? Why or why not?
- Would an LGBT couple or person be allowed to go on a mission trip?
- Does your church offer pastoral counseling, support groups, or other programs?
- What if a lesbian wanted to be baptized?

- Could an openly gay man join your church as a member?
- What would your staff do if an LGBT couple came to your church wanting to be married?
- What would the reaction be if a member had a sex change and still attended your church?
- If a man who had a sex change to be a woman started attending your church, could that person attend your women's ministry?
- Would an openly gay man be allowed to attend a men's retreat if he wanted to?
- What is the plan for the student ministry staff and volunteers when a teenager comes out or expresses same-sex attraction?
- How do you love and support LGBT teenagers who are in your church?
- Does your church have a plan to support parents whose kids have come out when the parents are unsure of how to respond?
- What happens when someone involved in your church comes out and sees no contradiction between homosexuality and God's laws in Scripture?
- Is your church a place where someone who has been in the LGBT community (but is currently not) can attend and be involved?
- Would your church be open to having dialogue with people from the LGBT community who aren't in your church?
- How does your pastor address LGBT issues in sermons?

Again, my point is not to suggest an answer to any of these questions. Rather, my question is this: Have churches sat down to have these conversations? If church leadership is willing to have these discussions, they are thinking on a different level than the leaders of most churches in America. Others in the church can push the leaders to have these conversations if they are not already doing so.

Churches should be having discussions like these on a regular basis. Why? Because the fight is worth it! The fight to bring people who aren't like you into your church and to have a church filled with people who are different from you is worth it! A church with messed-up people, a church with people who are struggling, a church with people who are searching for answers is *exactly* the kind of church you need. As many people have said before, church needs to be a place where you can "belong before you believe."

> Churches that ignore the issues of our current culture and stay in their safe bubble will eventually die—and they probably should.

Churches that ignore the issues of our current culture and stay in their safe bubble will eventually die—and they probably should. If you don't want that kind of church, become an advocate for change. Pray. Model the change you want to see. Respectfully but firmly keep pushing for holy messiness where you worship. You just might see your church becoming a body of people God uses to transform others for his glory.

You see, we don't create welcoming churches just to get along better with people from the gay community or other groups that make us uncomfortable. We want churches that love people and point them to Jesus.

There's going to come a time when you're able to share the gospel with LGBT people in your life. It will be difficult as you wrestle with grace and truth in your conversation. The truth side of the conversation will be especially hard. What will you say?

That's what the next chapter is all about.

REFLECTION AND DISCUSSION QUESTIONS

1. As you look at Luke 18:10–14, what are some ways that you can identify with both the tax collector and the Pharisee?
2. In what ways is the gospel of Jesus Christ messy? What does that mean?
3. Think about your church. Is there an atmosphere that would allow messy people to attend?
4. Why do you think some churches aren't willing to create an environment that attracts less-than-perfect people?
5. Look at the list of conversation questions near the end of this chapter. Start thinking through some of them. What scenarios would you have the toughest time with? Why?

Truth to Tell

It's funny that so many of us Christians say we want friends who are different from us so we can share Christ with them, but when we get them in our lives, we end up sending them away because we're too uncomfortable around them. Come to think of it, that's not funny at all. It's tragic.

A lot of Christians, especially Christian men, are uncomfortable around people from the LGBT community. And so they shun them. Or even worse. In cases like this, the label *homophobia*—fear of homosexuals—is justified.

Homophobia is not just a faux pas that can get people mad at you in today's social climate. Homophobia is a sin. It's being fearful of some of those for whom Jesus died and to whom he sent us to share the gospel—fearful of them to the point that we separate ourselves from them and give up any chance of influencing them for Jesus. In other words, homophobia is a form of spiritual discrimination, and we need to purge it from our midst.

The Bible tells us to fear two things: God and nothing. So don't fear people in the gay community—or anyone else for that matter. Seek people out and get to know them, and let them get to know you so that in time they can understand what God means to you. You may get a chance to tell an unbelieving person the good news that Jesus loves him or her. You might also get the chance for that person to have a positive impact on your life.

When you have a messy church supporting you, it's easier for you to approach people in the LGBT community with the gospel. If you attend a messy church, it becomes second nature to invite people to church because you know they'll be in an environment where they're not judged. But of course you may not attend a church that is messy—yet. Even in that case, though, you have the Holy Spirit with you to guide you and give you courage.

> Homophobia is not just a faux pas that can get people mad at you in today's social climate. Homophobia is a sin.

Several times in this book already, I've mentioned the importance of sharing the gospel with non-Christian people within the LGBT community. Now we're going to look at this issue squarely. I have some advice for you that you can use with people who may make you uncomfortable but whose lack of faith in Jesus continues to be a burden on your heart.

The most effective evangelism with people who make you feel uncomfortable takes place within the context of a relationship. This may be even more important for the LGBT community than for most others, since this is a community that has felt unheard, misunderstood, mistreated, and falsely characterized for years. (I think that many Christians have some apologizing to do to the LGBT community for social media rants, inappropriate jokes, street evangelizing signs, assumptions, and some for just being plain mean). So we must be sure to treat them as people, not as projects, and then point them to Jesus when possible.

The people we witness to may not ever embrace Jesus as Lord for themselves. But then again, they may.

Losing Vera

It was 2005. Several years had passed since I had graduated from Ozark Christian College. I had taken an associate pastor job with Shepherd Church in northern Los Angeles and was starting seminary at Talbot School of Theology at Biola University. My dad had finally come out to me as a gay man a couple of years earlier. I was shocked but processed through a lot of my emotions on the subject. By 2005, my parents and I seemed to be in a better place in regard to our relationship. I had also married my wonderful wife, Amy. I was in a great season of life where it seemed nothing could go wrong.

Then I got the phone call.

I couldn't believe what I was hearing over the phone. Vera was on the other end of the line, and she was telling me good-bye. Good-bye for what she believed would be the last time she would ever talk to me.

It wasn't a total surprise to me, but I hadn't known we'd already reached a place of such finality.

A few months earlier, Vera had been diagnosed with cancer, and it was serious. She was originally treated in Kansas City, and then she and my mother drove to Texas to try to get more advanced medical treatment. In the long run, though, it had seemed like the treatment offered at the clinic in Texas was going to be too much for Vera to handle. She told my mom that she was done fighting and was ready to go on to the "next world." My mother was crushed.

When they returned home, they set up their dining room as a hospice bedroom. Vera slept there, and most nights my mother slept in a chair next to her. Anytime Vera needed something in the middle of the night, my mother would get up and take care of it. This was a very difficult time for my mother. The woman she had loved and lived with for twenty-two years did not have much time left.

Vera's adult daughter also came to live with them during this time. They would often have visitors, people going back and forth to see how Vera was doing and to say good-bye. As the days went on, Vera got worse and worse as the cancer stole her memory and confused her mind. She was no longer the sharp woman she used to be.

Now Vera was on the phone with me, telling me good-bye for the last time. She assured me that I would see her "on the other side." I told Vera I would see her sooner than that because I was going to fly to Kansas City to say good-bye to her personally.

Right after I got off the phone, I went to my office at Shepherd and booked a round-trip ticket to Kansas City. Then I prayed. I made a deal with God. I told him that if he would open the door for me to talk to Vera, I would not go in there beating her over the head with a Bible like I did when I first came to faith. I began pleading with God to create an opportunity for me to talk to Vera about the gospel and to open her heart so she would be interested.

One Last Chance

Two days later, I kissed my wife good-bye and got on the plane. I flew out and stayed for five days.

My first day in Missouri, I tried to talk to Vera, but she was not very responsive. Even during the times when she was awake, she didn't say much. I don't know why, other than she wasn't feeling well and was probably not ready for me to start talking to her about Jesus. I would sit next to her for an hour at a time, and she would say nothing to me. Every now and then she would say, "Can you hand me a book, please?" She would then proceed to read with me sitting there, making no conversation whatsoever.

While my mission to tell Vera about the gospel one last time wasn't faring well, my conversations with my mother weren't much better. She was depressed and obviously feared the imminent. She told me over and over again that she had no idea what she was going to do without Vera or how she was going to make it through this transition. I wanted to get my mother out of the house so she could have a break and a change of scenery, but it was cold and snowing outside, so we couldn't go into town. Because my mother and Vera lived so far away from Kansas City, we were stuck at the house, with a lot of tension in the air and even more unanswered questions.

This was an introspective trip for me. I walked around the house, observing and thinking. I looked at the living room and re-called opening Christmas presents. I thought of parties Mom and Vera used to have in our house. I looked out front and remembered shooting off fireworks in the driveway. I remembered playing hide-and-seek with my cousins in the backyard. I went to my room and remembered how I used to stay up late and watch movies. I remem-bered the holidays we spent with Vera's family.

Many memories seemed to be floating around the house for me. And now a new, negative memory was being created with Vera slowly dying in the dining room.

I had been there for days, and God still hadn't given me an op-portunity to tell Vera about Jesus. I was tempted to just go up to her, grab her by her shoulders, and shake her until she understood the im-portance of the gospel. Instead, I waited on God and believed that he would provide an opportunity. On the last night I was there, I went and sat by her bed one last time, hoping she would wake up. She did!

She looked at me, knowing that I would be leaving the next day. I'm sure she knew this would be the last time we would ever talk. So she asked me one question. Her question shocked me.

"Caleb, what do you think is on the other side?"

Really? I mean, seriously, is there any better question than that? I was so excited.

"Jesus is on the other side!" I answered Vera. "If you submit to him as your Lord and Savior right now, he will carry you into the next life. All you have to do is repent, confess, and believe!"

I don't know what I was expecting at this point. Maybe I was expecting her to throw up her arms in excitement and sing "I Surrender All."

"You really want to know what I think about you and everyone who believes in Jesus?" Vera asked.

I knew what she thought, but still I answered, "Yes."

"I think you are weak. I think you and all the Christians you are around use Jesus as a crutch because you're not strong enough to make it through life on your own."

I suppose most Christians, hearing those words, would be bothered. They would take it as an insult. I took it as a compliment.

"Well, Vera, you're halfway to believing the gospel! You and I have to admit that we are weak and Jesus can make us strong. I *am* weak. And by the way, Jesus is not my crutch. He's my wheelbarrow! I'm not even in the backseat of his car; I'm in the trunk! I'm *not* strong enough to make it through this life on my own, so Jesus carries me. If you submit to him right now, he will take you as you are and he'll wipe away the pain and the hurt and the guilt from your life."

I honestly believed this was the moment when she would give her life to Jesus.

I was wrong.

She said she loved me, but she told me she wanted no part of Jesus.

I left the next morning, devastated.

The Emptiness of It All

A few days after I got back from seeing Vera for the last time, I was at a conference center in the mountains near our church, helping to lead a men's retreat. After the last session on Saturday night, I checked my voice mail. My mother had called and in tears left me a message that Vera had died.

I dropped my cell phone.

Although I had been expecting this news, when it came it seemed surreal to me. In an instant, I realized that Vera had passed from death into judgment, and unless a miracle had happened, she had gone before God without Jesus.

Tears began rolling down my face. Overwhelming feelings of sadness, guilt, anger, and depression hit me all at once. I didn't know what to do or how to react.

I went out into the lobby, where some of the other leaders of the retreat were standing around talking. My friend Scot saw me crying and immediately knew what had happened. He called the other guys together and they sat me down in a chair, where I began to sob uncontrollably. I was suffering from intense emotional pain that seemed to come out of nowhere.

At the same time, though, I had at least fifteen men surrounding me, laying hands on me, hugging me, and praying for me all at the same time. They stayed with me for over an hour while I cried. Not one guy left that room until I was ready to get up. Not one guy acted bored, but rather they surrounded me in prayer and comfort.

It was one of the most painful and gracious experiences I've ever had. And it helped me begin to adjust to the new reality.

A few days later, the funeral was held on the Plaza in downtown Kansas City. My wife and I, my wife's parents, and extended family of mine all flew out to Kansas City to attend the funeral. I was numb during the whole service. The funeral did not include worship, preaching, prayer, or anything else of a spiritual nature. Instead, it included a lot of people getting up and sharing memories about Vera. All of their memories were good.

I struggled for two reasons. First, not all of my memories of Vera were good. She had acted differently toward me than she had toward anyone else. Second, I struggled because, even though it was nice to hear the stories, no one shared any part of the gospel whatsoever. I was not asked to share anything, I think because my mom and the other funeral organizers knew I would talk about Jesus.

I was hurting because, in the long run, if Vera did not know who Jesus was, then all of the stories were just that: stories. What counted was who she knew on the other side of eternity. I still get sick to my stomach when I think about the possibility of her meeting God without Jesus at her side.

Nevertheless, even with all of the hard times Vera and I had, she was still a huge part of my life. I still miss her.

Through the years since, I've often reflected on my relationship with Vera. I've wanted to know where I went wrong in sharing the gospel with her. Did I do a bad job telling her about Jesus when I first came to Christ? Should I have stayed closer to home and been with her during her last days? To some degree, I am still plagued by these questions. How could I have done better?

He Saw the Person

To sharpen my skills in relating to people and sharing the gospel, I turned anew to Jesus's interactions with people. And I noticed something: Jesus loved everyone.

Even Samaritans.

The Jewish community did not look fondly on people from Samaria. The Samaritans were descendants of Israelites who had intermarried with foreign peoples. They also had some religious eccentricities that created tension between them and the Jewish people.

Then one day Jesus had an encounter in Samaria. He was headed north from Jerusalem and decided to go through Samaria instead of bypassing it like many Jews did. Around midday, when he got to the little town of Sychar, he sent his disciples to buy food while he had a seat beside the village well. Just then, a woman came to get some water from the well.

It's odd that a woman would come in the heat of the noonday. Most got water early in the morning or at night when it was cooler. Not her. As we will see, she had a past, so she probably went to the well at the time when it was least populated to avoid getting "those looks" or hearing "those comments" about herself.

Seeing her, Jesus asked for a drink. She was shocked.

The Samaritan woman said to him, "You are a Jew and I am a Samaritan woman. How can you ask me for a drink?" (For Jews do not associate with Samaritans.)

Jesus answered her, "If you knew the gift of God and who it is that asks you for a drink, you would have asked him and he would have given you living water." (John 4:9–10)

I love this. Jesus didn't care about the fact that she was a Samaritan, was a woman, or had a past. He broke all social norms to have an interaction that would result in her having a chance to come into discipleship with him.

The conversation went on.

> "Sir," the woman said, "you have nothing to draw with
> and the well is deep. Where can you get this living water?
> Are you greater than our father Jacob, who gave us the well
> and drank from it himself, as did also his sons and his
> livestock?"
>
> Jesus answered, "Everyone who drinks this water will be
> thirsty again, but whoever drinks the water I give them will
> never thirst. Indeed, the water I give them will become in
> them a spring of water welling up to eternal life."
>
> The woman said to him, "Sir, give me this water so that
> I won't get thirsty and have to keep coming here to draw
> water." (verses 11–15)

Up to this point, it had been a pleasant discussion—a little theological back-and-forth and a drink of water. How much deeper could it go? Well, Jesus took it there.

> He told her, "Go, call your husband and come back."
>
> "I have no husband," she replied.
>
> Jesus said to her, "You are right when you say you have
> no husband. The fact is, you have had five husbands, and the
> man you now have is not your husband. What you have just
> said is quite true." (verses 16–18)

This is what we call *busted*. Jesus knew her past and knew her list of honeys. Even though Jesus was going to end this conversation by letting this woman know who he really was and offering salvation to her, he was also letting her know that he knew things were not right at her house. This is a great example of grace *and* truth. The woman was obviously stunned by Jesus's knowledge of her:

> "Sir," the woman said, "I can see that you are a prophet. Our ancestors worshiped on this mountain, but you Jews claim that the place where we must worship is in Jerusalem."
>
> "Woman," Jesus replied, "believe me, a time is coming when you will worship the Father neither on this mountain nor in Jerusalem. You Samaritans worship what you do not know; we worship what we do know, for salvation is from the Jews. Yet a time is coming and has now come when the true worshipers will worship the Father in the Spirit and in truth, for they are the kind of worshipers the Father seeks. God is spirit, and his worshipers must worship in the Spirit and in truth." (verses 19–24)

I read what Jesus said here, and I notice a few things.

First, there is such a thing as good theology and bad theology. Jesus said the Samaritans were worshiping what they did not know. In other words, he said, "You're doing it wrong." This should leave a mental note for us that there is absolute truth in theology.

Second, Jesus said it is not the *place* that makes the worship but *who* you are worshiping. Again, Jesus upheld good theology. True worshipers worship in truth *and* Spirit! The two go hand in hand.

Jesus is the person we should put all of our worship focus on, not anyone else.

Third, I believe he was saying all of this to entice the woman to dive deeper into the conversation. He wasn't put off by what she'd done. Jesus didn't take a moment to chew her out as he was talking to her. He definitely wanted her to own her past, but her past did not have to keep her from him. He was drawing her in. She took the bait:

> The woman said, "I know that Messiah" (called Christ) "is coming. When he comes, he will explain everything to us."
>
> Then Jesus declared, "I, the one speaking to you—I am he." (verses 25–26)

Here this woman was claiming to know about the Messiah, and yet the Messiah was standing right in front of her. This must have been a huge revelation for her. I picture her dropping her water bucket and backing up, staring at him. Can't you see Jesus smiling in return? I've always thought Jesus had a sense of humor, and so he was probably looking at her in such a way as to say, *What are you going to do with this now?*

> Jesus is the person we should put all of our worship focus on, not anyone else.

When he saw this woman, he did not see her as somebody who made him feel uncomfortable. He did not identify her as somebody he had to work on. He did not view her as somebody who might take up too much of his time. He looked at her as a person—a person who needed to know God's love.

People or Projects?

You know what our tendency is? We befriend people who are not Christian and then treat them as our pet project. We unleash our evangelistic moves on them. The project then becomes scared, thinks we're weird, and runs.

Who can blame them? Being treated like a project is demeaning.

You know what a project is? Something you work on for a while before moving on. I know! I had science projects in high school that I would work on for a while and then toss aside. Sometimes you work really hard on projects; sometimes you don't. The common denominator is the fact that eventually you walk away from the project and focus on something else.

Have you ever been treated like a project? Do you like it when people seem to want to get to know you, and then you find out they are doing it just so they can sell insurance or a get-rich-quick product? It's not fun, and it makes you not want to trust them again. That's what our evangelistic methods feel like to unbelievers when we spring these tactics on them after a brief acquaintance.

I've shared the gospel with many people, and one of the things I've learned is that evangelism is not one-size-fits-all. We can't rely too heavily on our favorite method of evangelism. Any reasonable method (or no particular method at all) can work within the context of a caring relationship. The opposite is also true: without a relationship, our evangelism is likely to be ineffective, if not actually counterproductive.

If we refuse to get to know people on a deeper level because they make us uncomfortable, we may very well be sacrificing the opportunity to lead them to the Lord. I'm not saying we can never lead someone to the Lord without knowing him or her personally, but if we do know a person on some level, we should spend time getting to know who this person really is. That can only aid us in sharing the gospel.

How many of us are like Jesus and thrive on investing in people who are nothing like us? My guess is that not many of us are. People who are different from me are . . . well, different from me! But that does not mean we cannot get to know one another. That also doesn't mean we don't have anything in common. Finding points of contact is part of getting to know a person as a person and not as a project.

> Without a relationship, our evangelism is likely to be ineffective, if not actually counterproductive. If we refuse to get to know people on a deeper level because they make us uncomfortable, we may very well be sacrificing the opportunity to lead them to the Lord.

When we share Jesus with our new LGBT friends, we can never guarantee that they'll embrace him, any more than Vera did. However, we have to keep up our hope and be faithful in sharing Jesus to the best of our ability. In the end, the Lord does the work.

I want to continue with a little more of my personal story because it illustrates the surprising nature of the Holy Spirit, who is like a wind that "blows wherever it pleases" (John 3:8).

"I Think I Might Be Closer"

When Vera died, a huge part of my mother died with her. Mom seemed more vulnerable and somehow became more passive and uncertain of where to turn. Some of the people she thought were her friends dropped her like a bad habit. She was in and out of relationships with other women, some of whom emotionally or physically abused her. She slipped into a deep depression and started letting the house get trashy. This went on for a few years.

I tried to help my mom. Others did too. And slowly, so slowly, she began to pick up the pieces of her life.

One year Mom came to visit my family for Christmas. The day before she was going to head back to Kansas City, she attended Shepherd Church at our satellite campus, where I served as the campus pastor. On the way to the airport, I asked her what she thought of church the day before.

"Oh, it was very good. I really enjoyed it," my mom said. "I liked the way the pastor presented who Jesus was and what he did for us on the cross. I had never really heard anyone talk about Jesus like that."

I was a little ticked about this, to be honest with you. After all, I had been sharing the gospel with her in all kinds of creative ways over the years and she had never seemed to budge. But now she comes to our church campus, hears the senior pastor preach, and she gets interested . . . Oh well, it truly didn't matter whom she heard; I was just happy she had a good experience.

Oblivious of my feelings, Mom went on. "Caleb, after that sermon, I think I might be closer to making Jesus my Savior."

Right then I swerved into both lanes of traffic beside me, which allowed my mom to share a four-letter word right after she talked about Jesus.

But still . . .

Seriously? My mom had gotten to a place where she was actually thinking of Jesus? This was the same woman who had spent years trying to convince me that Christianity was a hoax. This was the same woman who had joined organizations just to make fun of Christianity, listened to Christian radio shows to criticize the preachers, was on the board of every organization she could think of that was anti-Christian, had told me there was no way she would ever support me becoming a pastor, and much more.

Now she was thinking of accepting Jesus?

Things were about to get interesting.

REFLECTION AND DISCUSSION QUESTIONS

1. Why do you think it was difficult for Vera to accept Jesus, even on her deathbed?
2. Have you ever known someone who died without knowing Jesus? What were the circumstances? How does that make you more passionate for those who don't know Jesus right now?
3. How do you see grace and truth at work in the John 4 story of the woman at the well?
4. What are some of the ways we end up treating people like projects?
5. How can we better ensure that we will treat people like people instead of projects? What are some things we can do?

A New ID

I've hinted at it before in the book, and now it's time to come out and say it: Christians need to stop trying to convert people's sexuality. It isn't our job to change someone's sexual orientation. You and I are not called by God to make gay people straight.

It is our job to lead anyone and everyone to Christ.

I believe God is big enough to deal with a person's sexuality.

Before some of you throw this book down in frustration, hear me out. I'm not saying we shouldn't call people to repentance. Absolutely we should! Everyone needs to repent and confess Christ. To go even further, I would say that repentance should be a spiritual discipline—something we do over and over again. There's a reason Jesus included a plea for forgiveness in the Lord's Prayer.

I'm also not saying we shouldn't urge people to turn from a sexual practice that God says in his Word is wrong. Yes, we should call all people to holy living after we share in a loving way what God has done for them in Jesus. We haven't done our full duty by them until we have taught them about obedience to God's commands in the Bible.

So once more, I'm not saying we shouldn't deal with repentance. I'm just saying we should consider whether we might be initially focusing on the wrong part of the issue when we are leading someone to Christ.

See, we get tangled up in the wrong arguments. The Bible talks about sexual intimacy being between a man and a woman, so we focus on people's morality instead of their spirituality—their sex life instead of their faith life. And then we get tangled up even further when we make the mistake of thinking that being gay is something we can tell people to just stop doing.

> Christians need to stop trying to convert people's sexuality. It isn't our job to change someone's sexual orientation. You and I are not called by God to make gay people straight.

We can tell people to stop stealing things, to stop cheating on their spouse, to stop looking at porn, to stop gossiping, and much more. As a pastor, I've carried out many counseling sessions with people in which I've told the counselees to stop a certain behavior. I myself have been in counseling and have been told to stop doing something (and I did stop).

Homosexuality is different.

It is more of an identity for the person than anything else. The person identifies as gay or lesbian and identifies with the LGBT community.

So we shouldn't try to make gay people straight. Instead, we should try to help people whose overriding identity is *LGBT* to become people whose overriding identity is *disciple*. They can replace a false identity with a true identity in Christ.

This point is crucial, and I've saved it for last because now you're ready for it. Now you're ready to have caring relationships with people from the LGBT community while having the right perspective about what's really important in it: discipleship. With this focus, you'll be ready to go out and influence others for Jesus. So let's dig into this idea more.

But first, I want to tell you the sequel to the story I opened the book with—the story of how nervous I was to preach on homosexuality with my parents in the crowd. My parents' faith experience can teach us a lot about what to keep

> We make the mistake of thinking that being gay is something we can tell people to just stop doing.

foremost in our minds and hearts when we share Christ with non-believers in the gay community.

The Rest of the Story

I stepped up to the stage and was ready to deliver my sermon. Mom and Dad were sitting in the back of the church where they normally sat, waiting to hear what I would say about homosexuality.

Every word of the sermon was difficult for me that day. I really felt as if I would get in trouble no matter what I said. If I talked about the truth, my parents and other people who identified as LGBT might get upset. If I started speaking on grace, some of the extreme Bible thumpers would get mad.

About a quarter of the way into the sermon, however, I made a mental note: I wasn't going to care about what people thought. I would just preach the tension of grace and truth and trust God to take care of the rest. He can handle messy.

After the sermon, I sheepishly went up to my parents, who were standing together in the lobby. They gave me reassuring smiles and hugged me. I was surprised to hear them praise the sermon. When I asked them why, they said, "Thanks for helping people think more about the LGBT community."

I walked out of church that day with my head held high.

A Welcome Party

So, just how did my parents start attending church?

Two years earlier I had left my previous church in the Los Angeles area, after serving there for eleven years, to become the senior pastor of a church in Dallas. Within a year of moving there, both of my parents moved to Dallas, separately.

My mom moved to Dallas before my dad, and when she did, something amazing happened. My wife and I had just started moving my mother's stuff into her new apartment when several members of our church showed up to welcome Mom and help us move her in. They knew about my mom's sexuality, and none of them cared. These people were just thrilled to have her there.

The next day my mom showed up for church. After the worship service, people crowded around her, eager to become her friends. Church members welcomed her into small groups and Sunday school classes. People invited her to parties and out to lunch. I stood back and watched God's people in action. It was in that moment that I knew some people in my church were developing a heart like Jesus's.

What a difference from the way my mom was treated at the church where I preached during college!

Nine months later, I found myself directing my dad down the freeway, as he had decided to move to Dallas too. He had retired from his job in Missouri, and he was eager to move to a new location. Just as I had done with my mom, I had found him an apartment to rent in the Dallas area. And the same thing happened for my dad that happened for my mom: church members showed up to move him in. They didn't care what he believed, what political party he was for, the fact that he was attracted to men—they were there to help out as much as they could.

What was even more incredible was that as time went on some church members were nicer to my parents than I was! I had never lived with both of my parents in the same town since I was a toddler, so this was a new adventure for me. There were many tense times between us. Some of it was my fault, some of it theirs, but we all tried hard. The consistency during that time came from some members of my church and how much they had learned to love people who were different from them.

Time passed. After three and a half years of serving in Dallas, I felt that God was prompting my family and me to pick up and move back to Southern California to lead Discovery Church. I had enjoyed serving in Dallas, and in many ways it was a hard decision to move. Probably the hardest part of it was sharing with my parents that I would be returning to Southern California. They would stay behind in Dallas.

An amazing thing happened two weeks before Amy and the kids and I left for California. In separate conversations I had with each of my parents, they both affirmed to me that they *believed in Jesus Christ and trusted him as Lord and Savior!*

I was floored.

My dad had gone to church, somewhat inconsistently, for years, but I wasn't sure whether he really believed. My mom never believed and, as I have described, was hostile to Christianity for a long time. After attending our Dallas church for almost three years, though, they both came to a place where they believed in Jesus.

How did this happen? To this day, I'm still not sure. I do believe that my parents are saved. I know they don't have all the same theological convictions I do, but I still believe they're saved. They exchanged an identity they had adopted for themselves over a period of many years and clung to Jesus Christ for their identity.

What's Your ID?

When I was a kid, I loved Superman. I still do. No matter who puts on the Superman outfit in the movies, my idea of Superman is always Christopher Reeve. When I was young and would watch him as Superman, I was puzzled about how no one could see that Clark Kent was really Superman. Seriously, no one could figure that out? When one was there, the other one was always gone.

There is actually this scene in *Superman III* where Superman gets hold of some Kryptonite with tar laced in it, and he becomes bad . . . really bad. Eventually Clark Kent steps out of the bad Superman and they fight. Who is he fighting? Himself? Of course Clark wins, and then he opens his shirt, revealing the Superman emblem. You can't separate Clark Kent and Superman because Superman's identity is Clark Kent and vice versa.

Similarly, in the past when I've talked to my parents about telling people they're gay or lesbian, they've said they see it as their identity—who they are. In their minds, they couldn't separate their identity from their sexuality. That's very common among the people I know who are LGBT. So, when you and I tell people to stop being gay, they hear that as giving up their identity. If you and I think that just telling someone to stop being gay will put an end to that desire, we are dead wrong. It shows no understanding of how people in this community see themselves.

Don't ever ask me how I learned this (because I don't remember and don't want to remember), but my mom and Vera were not intimate during the last several years of their relationship. Yet they still identified themselves as lesbians. How can that be? Maybe the answer is that for them homosexuality wasn't as much about who they had sex with as it was about what they believed in, the movement they identified with, and the community they belonged to.

When most Christians tell someone in the gay community "Stop being gay," what they really mean is "Stop having sex with someone of the same gender." Yet here's what the person who is gay might think: *You want me to give up my feelings, partner, friends, cause, movement, community, and more.* Being gay is so much more than just who they have sex with—it's about friends, community, a cause, and deep feelings. It's about identity.

That may not make sense to you at first, but consider it for a moment.

All of us to some extent have created a false identity for ourselves. Most people describe themselves by what they do (work), who they are related to (family), or what they identify with (behavior). Some people's identity is shaped by their pain or addiction. Some are all about their causes. These kinds of things become the source of our self-made identities. We create false (or at least incomplete) identities for ourselves without even trying.

Before some take offense at where they think I'm going with this line of thinking, let me say that I understand there are many LGBT people who say they have had same-sex attraction since they can remember. Not everyone in the LGBT community was abused, molested, made fun of, or beaten up as a kid. Christians need to realize that some people are attracted to the same gender and there doesn't seem to be a clear reason why. I'm not sure that some people have control of whom they're attracted to. Maybe some do. I've met a lot of people in the LGBT community who say they were born gay, and I've met others who said that they weren't born that way. Regardless, my point is that some people in the LGBT community tend to rely on something other than Christ to define themselves. Just like everybody else does.

Coming to Christ, though, means we no longer identify ourselves as anything other than a disciple. It's why Paul said in Ephesians 4:22–24, "You were taught, with regard to your former way of life, to put off your old self, which is being corrupted by its deceitful desires; to be made new in the attitude of your minds; and to put on the new self, created to be like God in true righteousness and holiness."

> Every person in one way or another needs to exchange a false identity he or she has created for an identity in the risen Christ.

Old self to new self. Through Christ, we fundamentally change. Our identity is first and foremost as a disciple of Jesus. We are not to be

- gay Christians
- straight Christians
- conservative Christians
- liberal Christians
- contemporary Christians
- liturgical Christians
- free church Christians
- missional Christians
- any other adjective Christians

We are disciples. Before anything else, we follow Jesus. Our identity is in no one and nothing else. So our mission is to help people trade the identity they have created for Christ's identity. That's true for all of us:

- The angry person needs to exchange rage for grace through Christ.
- The worrier needs to switch from worry to trust in Christ.
- The porn addict needs to replace lust with love for Christ.
- The gossiper needs to exchange gossip for prayer to Christ.
- The control freak needs to swap control with reliance on Christ.
- The depressed one needs to find joy in Christ.
- The fearful person needs to discover confidence through Christ.

Every person in one way or another needs to exchange a false identity he or she has created for an identity in the risen Christ. Saying we're a disciple and a [fill in the blank] creates a big problem. At the level of our fundamental identity, we are a disciple *only*. I understand that we might define ourselves by our work, as a spouse, as a parent, or by other things—but at the core level of our existence, we are a disciple of Jesus.

I don't think the early Christian leaders identified themselves in any other way. I mean, can you imagine?

- Paul says, "I'm the first Reformed Christian."
- John says, "I'm the first touchy-feely Christian."
- Peter says, "I'm the first political Christian."

- James says, "I'm the first conservative Christian."
- Andrew says, "I'm the first seeker-sensitive Christian."
- Thomas says, "I'm the first skinny jeans Christian."

Here's what I believe when it comes to identity: God never created sexuality to define us. God never intended family, work, politics, sports teams, hobbies, and the like to define us. God created us *for* himself, to be defined *by* himself. When we choose to be defined by these other things in our life instead of Christ, we're not just creating a false identity—we're also committing idolatry. God wants our main identity to be a disciple of Jesus.

The apostles identified themselves as disciples and didn't add much to it, though they may have had to deal with the disciple-plus phenomenon in the churches where they served. I say that because of what Paul wrote to the Corinthians:

> One of you says, "I follow Paul"; another, "I follow Apollos"; another, "I follow Cephas"; still another, "I follow Christ."
>
> Is Christ divided? Was Paul crucified for you? Were you baptized in the name of Paul? I thank God that I did not baptize any of you except Crispus and Gaius, so no one can say that you were baptized in my name. (Yes, I also baptized the household of Stephanas; beyond that, I don't remember if I baptized anyone else.) For Christ did not send me to baptize, but to preach the gospel—not with wisdom and eloquence, lest the cross of Christ be emptied of its power.
> (1 Corinthians 1:12–17)

The temptation to create divisions around secondary identities may be as old as the church. But it's always wrong.

Your identity is disciple.

So it is of any gay or lesbian person who comes to Christ through grace.

Gay People in Heaven?

Here's a question I get asked a lot: "Can someone be LGBT and go to heaven?"

The answer? Yes!

Let me make a couple of points here. First of all, same-sex attraction is *temptation* to sin; it's not sin in itself. If temptation were sin, then that means Jesus sinned when he was tempted in the wilderness for forty days. But nowhere in Scripture does it say that being tempted is sinful. Now, if someone tempted by same-sex attraction indulges lustful thoughts or physically acts out on his or her sexual desires, that is a sin. But by itself, the attraction is only a temptation, not a sin. And therefore, even if same-sex temptation remains persistent, that is no evidence whatsoever that someone has not been accepted by God.

Second, we rely on grace through faith in Jesus, not on our performance, for our hope in heaven. So even if someone does give in to same-sex temptation and commits sin, that doesn't disqualify him or her from heaven if this person is in a relationship with Jesus. The sin is sad, to be sure. It might have harmful consequences. It might call for discipline from God. But a person who is in Christ and commits a sin has been forgiven and can be forgiven again. All Christians in heaven will be less-than-perfect people who sinned before and after salvation.

Can someone be gay and go to heaven? I think if we're going to ask that question, then we have to ask if someone can be an alcoholic and go to heaven. Can someone be addicted to drugs and go to heaven? Can someone be a gossip and go to heaven? Can someone be a worrier and go to heaven? Can someone be jealous of others and go to heaven? Can someone be an arrogant know-it-all Christian and go to heaven? [13]

Most Christians I know wouldn't have an issue with saying that any one of those people could go to heaven, but for some reason, when it comes to homosexuality, some think that is too tall of an order for God. I think it's because their view of God is too small. He's calling everyone into his kingdom all the time, as hard as that may be for us to believe.

> The Christian community needs to own the fact that people are deep, struggles are real, and people are working through them.

So let's note some distinctions. There is a difference between someone who identifies as LGBT and is sold out to Jesus and someone who is LGBT and isn't following Christ. There's a difference between someone who's honestly struggling to understand and accept what the Bible says about the issue of homosexuality and someone who doesn't care what the Bible has to say. There's a difference between a Christian who is trying to be sexually pure but slips up occasionally and someone who is freely indulging her same-sex passions. There is a difference between a Christian who is in a same-sex relationship searching for God at the same time and someone who doesn't care about God whatsoever. These are big differences, and we need to acknowledge them. The Christian community needs to own the fact that people are deep, struggles are real, and people are working through them.

What about those who say they love Jesus, claim to believe in the Bible, and attend church regularly and meanwhile are in a loving gay relationship? Are they saved? What should our reaction be?

I'm not sure we are supposed to be the judges of others' salvation. That matter is between them and God. I do think, however, that we can be discerning of the fruit that others are bearing. Consistent resistance to living for God, whether in regard to sexual morality or something else, should be concerning. We don't need to judge. But if conversations on sexuality come up and we have the standing with a person to talk about it, then we should graciously stand for what God's Word says. That's not because we're busybodies but because we want what's best for the other.

Sure, it's messy. We have to recognize there are people who are Christian and have sexual tension, and they will live in that tension for the rest of their lives. They will deal with the struggle between what God says in his Word and what they feel. Paul outlined this kind of struggle in Romans 7:15–20:

> I do not understand what I do. For what I want to do I do
> not do, but what I hate I do. And if I do what I do not want
> to do, I agree that the law is good. As it is, it is no longer I
> myself who do it, but it is sin living in me. For I know that
> good itself does not dwell in me, that is, in my sinful nature.
> For I have the desire to do what is good, but I cannot carry it
> out. For I do not do the good I want to do, but the evil I do
> not want to do—this I keep on doing. Now if I do what I do
> not want to do, it is no longer I who do it, but it is sin living
> in me that does it.

Please understand that I am in no way, shape, or form making excuses for people who live contrary to what they know God's Word says. My point is simply this: people are complex, and we need to seek to understand them in a relationship before we make assumptions about them. Individually and in our churches, we have to be willing to walk journeys with one another and learn how to listen as we embrace the tension of grace and truth. We need to know that for some people it will be a lifelong journey that will be messy, but they need people to walk with them.

Carlton's Identity

As disciples, we need to let people know that God does not hate them but loves them. God is not mad at them. Rather, he is mad *for* them! I truly believe we need to help people—no matter what sins they have committed—to replace their identity with Christ's identity. Let me give you an example of what I mean.

When I first came to California, I had a friend named Carlton. He was a tall, fun-loving guy who was in his midthirties at the time. He was involved in our church's singles ministry, Bible studies, and praise teams. Then our church had an opening in our finance department, and Carlton decided to apply for the job. He was one of the smartest people I knew when it came to numbers, and he got the position.

We went out to lunch one day to celebrate his new job, and while we were at lunch, he looked at me and said, "Caleb, I don't know if you know this or not, but I am gay. I'm not in a relationship right now, but I still have these desires and feelings." I don't know whether Carlton knew this or not (he probably did), but his news was not a shock to me. I had seen the signs.

Carlton looked at me and said, "Do you know what's different about you, Caleb? You don't treat me like a leper. You don't treat me like someone who is horrible. You treat me as a friend."

He went on to tell me that so many people in his life who claimed to be Christians acted very differently. He felt they didn't want anything to do with him once they found out he was gay. Before he found Shepherd Church, he was beginning to feel like he would have to go to a church where the Bible was watered down.

Near the end of my lunch with Carlton, he shared his belief that because of what he had come to know about the Bible, it wasn't right for him to act out on his same-sex attractions. He knew he would not be able to change his feelings on his own, and he even said, "I don't know if I'll ever be able to change. I believe that the answer for me is celibacy. God will give me the strength to live for him. When I die, I may still have gay feelings and I may still be attracted to men. But because I believe what Scripture says about homosexuality, giving up my sexual activity is a small price to pay compared to what Jesus did for me on the cross."

> God is not mad at them. Rather, he is mad *for* them!

I was blown away. Here was a guy who openly said that same-sex attraction was something he struggled with, yet he was willing to live for God. How many people do you know like that? How many people do you know with any kind of struggles who say, "I love God more than I love my sin, so I'm going to choose to love God and live for him"? That's pretty amazing.

Carlton got very sick after he started working at the church. He ended up going to the hospital shortly before I moved to Texas. We continued to speak on the phone often. I still remember how Carlton called me from the hospital one day and said he was ready to go and be with his Father. Soon after that conversation, Carlton closed his eyes and never reopened them.

I was privileged to be able to go back to California to preach at his funeral. It was incredible to see how many people were touched by his life. It was encouraging to see a huge congregation of people from Shepherd Church and some people from the LGBT community of Los Angeles coming together to worship God and to remember the life of Carlton. God used Carlton's life to bring together people on opposite sides of the argument for a time of celebration. That memorial service was a living illustration of grace and truth. I'm sure Carlton, if he was looking on from heaven, was pleased to see his life used in that way.

I know that right up until the time Carlton died, he still struggled with his sexuality, but he went to be with the Lord. Carlton illustrated the point to me that it doesn't matter who you are—if you really give your life to Jesus, you are covered by grace, and Jesus is bigger than any lifestyle we could ever live. There's a big difference between someone like Carlton who says, "I have these feelings, but I choose to live for Christ" and someone who says, "I have these feelings, and I'm going to live my life the way I want, no matter what God's Word says."

Again, we can say that for any sin, right?

Disciples Together

I was proud of Shepherd Church for how much they loved Carlton.

I was proud of some of the people in Texas for how much they loved my parents.

I'm also proud of my current church, Discovery Church, and how they have a heart to be a church that unchurched people love to attend.

I think these churches and many other churches around the

country understand that we can love people even though we don't agree with them. Situations can get messy, but if we refuse to give up either grace or truth, God will do something great in our midst. People who are in the LGBT community can go from being "them" to being our friends. People whose primary identity starts out as *gay* can replace that with the primary identity of *disciple*. After all, none of us could hope for any greater privilege than being a disciple of such a Master.

I hope more of my fellow Christians will now begin to live in the tension of grace and truth, give up their fear, break down the barriers, and form relationships of love and compassion with people from the LGBT community.

Just as Jesus would.

REFLECTION AND DISCUSSION QUESTIONS

1. According to this chapter, why is the subject of identity so important to this topic?
2. Why do we create false identities for ourselves? How can we break down these false identities in exchange for Jesus?
3. Does Carlton's story give you hope? How does it give you hope?
4. Read 1 Corinthians 1:12–17. What was Paul's main point in this passage? How do we see this playing out in today's world? How can we apply what Paul said here to our everyday lives?
5. What false identity have you created for yourself that needs to be broken down? Why was this identity created? Spend some time in prayer asking God to tear it down for you.

A Final Word

I have no doubt that many will disagree with some of the things I have written in this book. That's completely okay with me because I'm still thinking through these issues and striving to make sure my opinions are grounded in Scripture. Anyway, I didn't write this book to tell you what to think. I wrote this book to share my heart with you and hopefully help you think at a deeper level about this issue.

It is not all black and white, though I completely support what the Bible says about sexual intimacy. There's tension for people on both sides of this issue. Anytime you have people involved in a situation, it gets complicated. It is filled with pain, regret, hurt, growth, joy, and more.

I want you to struggle in the tension of grace and truth. Just like I do.

My strongest desire for you is to get messy in the lives of other people, no matter who they are. Because the outcome, by God's doing, is God's love blooming in many people's lives.

While I'm being open with you, I must confess that I'm still journeying with my parents, and our relationships are not easy ones.

We are still working out many issues. But I believe God has their hearts. They were both totally in favor of this book, and I'm excited that they see God using this story to help others.

Both of my parents are Christians now, which still amazes me. Do they believe in Jesus? Yes. Are they Christian? Yes. Do they still struggle with same-sex attraction? Yes. (They were both in the gay community for thirty years or more—it doesn't just turn off.) Do they believe exactly as I do on every theological issue? No. Do some Christians still judge them? Probably. Will they mess up? Yes. Does that mean they are not saved? No. Are they going to church? When they can. Is God with them on the path they are walking? Yes.

How do all of these things go together? I don't know.

It's messy.

It's all part of the tension between grace and truth.

I just know that God has called me to live in grace and truth, preaching both. And he understands the tension ... completely. That's enough for me.

I want to leave you with one of my favorite verses, which should guide our ministry and theology on this issue. It's John 13:35:

> By this everyone will know that you are my disciples, *if you love one another.*

Acknowledgments

Gene Appel. Thanks for taking an interest in me since I returned to Southern California. You've helped me think through ministry and personal life matters. You're a true leader.

Mike Baker. One talk with you in high school and now I'm a pastor. You still impact me.

David and Tracey Buster. Thanks for loving me in high school and still believing in me today. You both mean a lot to me.

Ben Cachiaras. Thank you for showing me that one can be a pastor and a scholar at the same time.

Barry Cameron. Thanks for the wisdom and words of truth you've spoken into my life. It has changed me and challenged me.

Kye S. Chung. Thanks for being someone who is a faithful friend and has my back. You make ministry happen.

Todd Clark. You've been a friend and coach through my ministry years. Thanks for being a safe place.

Doug Crozier. Thank you for seeing in me what others never could. Your support has seen me through good and rough times.

Trevor DeVage. You've become a good friend to share and bounce ideas with. Thank you.

Mike Foster. Two days with you changed my life. I'm honored to still do life with you.

Patrick Garcia. My close friend with whom I can be real.

Don Gates. Without you, this book would have never happened. You're amazing. The journey has only begun.

Rusty George. You've been a faithful friend since I returned to the area. It's good to have a like-minded person nearby.

Jack Graham. Thank you for your mentorship and reaching across aisles. Love you!

Andy Hansen. Thanks for investing in me back then and even into today. Your living room is still my home.

Tim Harlow. You still believe in my uniqueness and call. You invite me to conversations and couches and give me a place at the table. It means a lot.

Kyle Idleman. You've always been a cheerleader for me and for this story, ever since our college days. Thank you.

Gregg Jennings. You baptized me and started me on my journey. I love you, man, and I'm so proud of you. Along these lines, thanks also to my two other good high school friends, Big Jon and Phil. The four of us have had some amazing times together.

Max Jennings. You were the first pastor I heard preach the gospel. Thank you.

Cal Jernigan. Thank you for encouraging me, inviting me to your circle, and reminding me that family is first.

Brian Jobe. Thanks for encouraging me every step of the way. You make rough roads smoother.

Jason and Seana Scott. Words can't express what you two mean to me.

John Latvatalo. You stood by my side and believed in me.

Mark Moore. You were my first spiritual father. I'm proud to be one of your sons. The hawk is soaring.

Dale Penn. You're still my best man.

Dave and Julia Rossen. Thanks for always looking out for our family and for loving us.

Bob Russell. Even though I was never one of your interns, I feel

I've been grafted in. Thanks for your influence in my life. There are still giants in the land.

Dudley Rutherford. You gave me chances and always stand in my corner. I love you, Coach.

Drew Sherman. You were the pastor I needed during a dark period in my life. I'm grateful for you.

Robin Sigars. I still remember that CIY sermon, and I'm still filling those shoes.

Matt Summers. You've been my friend since college. Thank you for joking with me, keeping me humble, and most of all, for supporting me as your friend.

Jud Wilhite. You've been a friend and mentor since 1998. You model radical grace. I consider *you* my pastor.

Tim Winters. You were first my boss, then my mentor, and now you are one of my best friends. You're always an inspiration.

Also, thank you to . . .

The WaterBrook Multnomah team. Alex Field, Amy Haddock, David Kopp, Stephen Reed, Beverly Rykerd, Eric Stanford, Susan Tjaden, Laura Wright, and others. Your team embodies excellence. Love you all.

My Southern California pastors. Gene Appel, John Amstutz, Chuck Booher, Mike Breaux, Rob Denton, Ian DiOrio, Kevin Haah, Mike and Jodi Hickerson, Tom Hughes, Mike Johnson, Scott Julian, Glenn Kirby, Rick Kyle, Ken LaMont, David Macer, Chris Nicely, John Scott, Frank Sontag, Tim Spivey, Albert Tate, Shawn Thornton, Jeff Vines, Jeff Walling, Shane Womack—I feel like we are all on the same team here in SoCal. I love doing ministry with you.

Some of my fellow pastor friends. Rick Atchley, Brandon Bradley, Aaron Brockett, James Brummett, Arron Chambers, Bo

Chancey, Bruce Cramer, Jason Cullum, Charlie Curran, Ben Davis, Dave Dummitt, Glen Elliot, Dave Flaig, David Garison, Dave Hamlin, John Hampton, Jerry Harris, Cam Huxford, Ken Idleman, Gary Johnson, Greg Johnson, Darrell Land, Greg Lindsey, Tim Liston, Eddie Lowen, Hal Miner, Mont Mitchell, Bryan Morrow, Shan Moyers, Frank Nichols, Kevin Odor, David Patrick, Chris Philbeck, Shane Philip, Steve Poe, George Powell, Steve Reeves, George Ross, Rick Rusaw, David Rutherford, Casey Scott, Chris Seidman, John Seitz, Rick Shonkwiler, Jamie Snyder, Dave Stone, Roger Storms, Scott Sutherland, Jim Tune, Jon Weece, Don Wilson. You guys are my brothers. I love you guys.

My preaching mentors. Scott Barfoot, Kent Edwards, Matt Proctor, Roger Raymer, Haddon Robinson, Mark Scott, Don Sunukjian, Timothy Warren. You taught me how to communicate the gospel with grace and truth.

The Discovery Church elder team, staff team, and members. Thank you for believing in this project and in our church: love God, love people. Special thanks to my assistant and friend, Cathy Schroeder, who kept me on track. I'm blessed to work with you.

Those who helped me think through the story. Anneke Bernardo, Jason and Jody Brazelton, Virgil Brown, Scott and Christine Curtis, Mark Dever, Matt and Sarah Lynn Grubb, Margie Ings, Lane Jones, Irene Kendrick, Sean McDowell, Angie Merrill, Laura Milner, Natalie Pawlik, Scott Rae, James Schaffner, Joe Smith, Thom Stark, Matt Summers, Lu Williams, Joe Wright. Thank you for valuable feedback.

Notes

1. I understand that in recent times the acronym has been updated to LGBTQ or LGBTQIA, but for the sake of those I am referring to in this book, I have chosen to use LGBT since I am mainly talking about lesbian, gay, bisexual, and transgendered people.
2. Hector is a composite figure. I have known many people with stories much like Hector's.
3. The story in John 7:53–8:11 does not appear in the earliest manuscripts of the gospel of John, so it may not originally have been in there. But it has all the hallmarks of Jesus and is probably a true story from his life.
4. I think it should be noted, however, that contrary to the view of some Christians, many in the gay community are *not* part of the political machine.
5. For a similar event, see Judges 19:22–24.
6. John Stott, *Romans* (Downers Grove, IL: InterVarsity Press, 1994), 78.
7. For further study on the Romans 1 passage, I recommend the following sources: James D. G. Dunn, *Romans 1–8,* Word Biblical Commentary, vol. 38A, ed. Bruce M. Metzger (Nashville: Thomas Nelson, 1988); Douglas Moo, *The Epistle to the Romans,* The New International Commentary on the New Testament (Grand Rapids, MI: Eerdmans, 1996); Leon Morris,

The Epistle to the Romans, The Pillar New Testament Commentary (Grand Rapids, MI: Eerdmans, 1988); and Thomas R. Schreiner, *Romans,* Baker Exegetical Commentary on the New Testament (Grand Rapids, MI: Baker Academic, 1998).

8. The Greek word is *porneia,* used in Matthew 5:32.

9. Sarah N. Lynch and Kim Palmer, "Republican Senator with Gay Son Now Backs Gay Marriage," *Reuters,* March 15, 2013, www.reuters.com/article/2013/03/15/us-usa-portman -gaymarriage-idUSBRE92E0G020130315.

10. The first Bell quote is taken from "Interview: Why Rob Bell Supports Gay Marriage," YouTube video, 2:47, posted by OdysseyNetworks, March 20, 2013, www.youtube.com/ watch?v=-q0iDaW6BnE. The next two Bell quotes are taken from "Rob Bell Affirms Homosexuality," YouTube video, 1:33, posted by "Justin Hoke," March 18, 2013, www.youtube.com/ watch?v=Wb83v4P2yS0.

11. For more on celibacy, see Jenell Williams Paris, *The End of Sexual Identity: Why Sex Is Too Important to Define Who We Are* (Downers Grove, IL: InterVarsity Press), 2011, and Eve Tushnet, *Gay and Catholic: Accepting My Sexuality, Finding Community, Living My Faith* (Notre Dame, IN: Ave Maria Press), 2014.

12. R. T. France, *The Gospel of Matthew,* The New International Commentary on the New Testament (Grand Rapids, MI: Eerdmans, 2007), 725–26.

13. I understand that people who identify as LGBT cringe at the idea of being compared to addicts, gossipers, and such. But my argument here is for the sake of saying that God's grace is bigger than what any of us could imagine.

More Reading

Many books have been written about homosexuality from a Christian perspective, taking all kinds of angles. The following are a few I recommend for anyone who wants to learn more about the subject.

Allberry, Sam. *Is God Anti-Gay? And Other Questions About Homosexuality, the Bible, and Same-Sex Attraction.* Purcellville, VA: The Good Book Company, 2013.

Barr, Adam T., and Ron Citlau. *Compassion Without Compromise: How the Gospel Frees Us to Love Our Gay Friends Without Losing the Truth.* Minneapolis: Bethany House, 2014.

Brown, Michael L. *Can You Be Gay and Christian? Responding with Love and Truth to Questions About Homosexuality.* Lake Mary, FL: Frontline, 2014.

Butterfield, Rosaria Champagne. *Secret Thoughts of an Unlikely Convert: An English Professor's Journey into Christian Faith.* Pittsburgh, PA: Crown and Covenant, 2012.

DeYoung, Kevin. *What Does the Bible Really Teach About Homosexuality?* Wheaton, IL: Crossway, 2015.

Gagnon, Robert A. J. *The Bible and Homosexual Practice: Texts and Hermeneutics.* Nashville: Abingdon, 2002.

Hill, Welsley. *Washed and Waiting: Reflections on Christian Faithfulness and Homosexuality.* Grand Rapids: Zondervan, 2010.

McDowell, Sean, and John Stonestreet. *Same-Sex Marriage:*

A Thoughtful Approach to God's Design for Marriage. Grand Rapids, MI: Baker, 2014.

Paris, Jenell Williams. *The End of Sexual Identity: Why Sex Is Too Important to Define Who We Are.* Downers Grove, IL: InterVarsity Press, 2011.

Platt, David. *Counter Culture: A Compassionate Call to Counter Culture in a World of Poverty, Same-Sex Marriage, Racism, Sex Slavery, Immigration, Persecution, Abortion, Orphans, and Pornography.* Carol Stream, IL: Tyndale, 2015. (Especially chapters 6 and 7.)

Tushnet, Eve. *Gay and Catholic: Accepting My Sexuality, Finding Community, Living My Faith.* Notre Dame, IN: Ave Maria Press, 2014.

Yuan, Christopher, and Yuan, Angela. *Out of a Far Country: A Gay Son's Journey to God. A Broken Mother's Search for Hope.* Colorado Springs: WaterBrook, 2011.

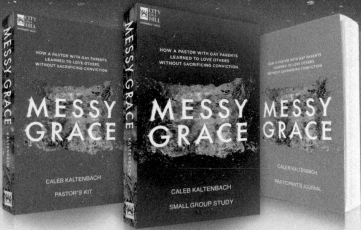